At Issue

Sexual Assault and the Military

Other Books in the At Issue Series

At Issue

Sexual Assault and the Military

Noah Berlatsky, Book Editor

GREENHAVEN PRESS
A part of Gale, Cengage Learning

GALE
CENGAGE Learning·

Farmington Hills, Mich • San Francisco • New York • Waterville, Maine
Meriden, Conn • Mason, Ohio • Chicago

GALE
CENGAGE Learning

Patricia Coryell, *Vice President & Publisher, New Products & GVRL*
Douglas Dentino, *Manager, New Products*
Judy Galens, *Acquisitions Editor*

For more information, contact:
Greenhaven Press
27500 Drake Rd.
Farmington Hills, MI 48331-3535
Or you can visit our Internet site at gale.cengage.com

Articles in Greenhaven Press anthologies are often edited for length to meet page requirements. In addition, original titles of these works are changed to clearly present the main thesis and to explicitly indicate the author's opinion. Every effort is made to ensure that Greenhaven Press accurately reflects the original intent of the authors. Every effort has been made to trace the owners of copyrighted material.

Cover photograph copyright © Images.com/Corbis.

LIBRARY OF CONGRESS CATALOGING-IN-PUBLICATION DATA

Sexual assault and the military / Noah Berlatsky, book editor.
        pages cm. -- (At issue)
    Includes bibliographical references and index.
    ISBN 978-0-7377-7187-9 (hardcover) -- ISBN 978-0-7377-7188-6 (pbk.)
    1. United States--Armed Forces--Women--Crimes against. 2. United States--Armed Forces--Women--Violence against. 3. Soldiers--United States--Crimes against. 4. Rape--United States. 5. Rape--Law and legislation--United States. 6. Military offenses--United States. I. Berlatsky, Noah, editor.
    UB418.W65S42 2015
    364.15'32088355--dc23
                                                                    2014033869

Printed in the United States of America
1 2 3 4 5   19 18 17 16 15

Contents

Introduction

The Tailhook scandal occurred more than twenty years ago, but it remains an iconic example of the problems with sexual assault in the military.

The Tailhook Association is a fraternal organization for naval pilots. Every year it holds a symposium, or convention. After the thirty-fifth annual symposium, in 1991, Navy lieutenant Paula Coughlin reported to her superior officer that she had been forced to run down a hallway where she was groped and fondled by as many as two hundred men. The admiral was not helpful; in fact he told her, "That's what you get when you go down a hallway full of drunk aviators."[1] He took no action, and Coughlin eventually went to the press.

As the scandal unfolded, it became clear that Coughlin was far from the only one attacked at the convention. Eighty-seven women reported assaults at Tailhook. Some of these women were military personnel, like Victim #7, a Navy lieutenant who was repeatedly touched and groped by men who placed squadron stickers on her body.[2] Some were civilians, like Victim #9, a bartender who was groped, insulted, and even bitten while she tried to serve drinks. There were also reports of seven male officers being groped, in some cases by women.

Victim #7 noted that she had been assaulted in the same hallway where Coughlin was attacked. However, according to her testimony, "She believed that the 'brass' knew about the harassment and lewd behavior toward women in the hallway at Tailhook '90 and assumed they would address the behavior. Thus, she did not report her assault nor anything she saw to

---

1. Quoted in Jennifer Hlad, "Tailhook Whistle-blower Wants Congressional Hearing on Lackland," *Stars and Stripes*, August 1, 2012. http://www.stripes.com/news/navy/tailhook-whistle-blower-wants-congressional-hearing-on-lackland-1.184595.
2. *Frontline*, "Tailhook: Victim Number 7," February 1993. http://www.pbs.org/wgbh/pages/frontline/shows/navy/tailhook/vic07.html.

any higher authority."[3] Another witness, Victim #38, said that she too knew the hallway was "crazy" from earlier conventions.[4] The harassment Coughlin experienced, then, does not seem to have been a one-time incident but a regular and accepted part of the yearly Tailhook convention.

The Tailhook scandal had a major impact on the US Navy. The officer Coughlin accused directly was not convicted, and it is believed that she misidentified him. However, "the careers of fourteen admirals and almost 300 naval aviators were scuttled or damaged by Tailhook," according to a report by the PBS series *Frontline*.[5] Secretary of the Navy H. Lawrence Garrett III was forced to resign. The Tailhook conventions (their name changed to "symposiums") have been "more subdued," according to *The Washington Post*, and Navy aviators have attempted to change their reputation for drinking and "outdated attitudes toward women."[6]

However, many worry that the Tailhook scandal did not actually change the military in a fundamental way, and that a culture of tolerance for sexual abuse and harassment still persists. In 2013, the Pentagon released a report indicating that more than twenty-six thousand military personnel were sexually assaulted in 2012. In addition, the Air Force officer in charge of dealing with sexual harassment and assault was himself arrested on charges of sexually assaulting a woman in a parking lot. The president of the Tailhook Association, Captain Gregory McWherter, was also accused in 2014 of encouraging and condoning harassment and misconduct in the Blue Angels, an elite Navy flight squadron under his command.

3. *Ibid.*
4. *Frontline*, "Tailhook: Victim Number 38," February 1993. http://www.pbs.org/wgbh /pages/frontline/shows/navy/tailhook/vic38.html.
5. *Frontline*, "Post Tailhook Punishment," accessed September 22, 2014. http://www .pbs.org/wgbh/pages/frontline/shows/navy/tailhook/disc.html.
6. Craig Whitlock, "Accused Navy Pilot Gregory McWherter Resigns as Tailhook Association President," *Washington Post*, April 25, 2014. http://www.washingtonpost.com /world/national-security/accused-navy-pilot-gregory-mcwherter-resigns-as-tailhook -association-president/2014/04/25/f712470c-cca5-11e3-a75e-463587891b57_story .html.

And finally there have been recent accusations that basic training instructors systematically harassed and abused trainees at the Lackland Air Force Base in San Antonio, Texas.

John Lehman, former secretary of the Navy, has argued that Tailhook was "a grotesquely disproportionate witch hunt," and that the problems with sexual harassment in the military are not as serious as they are made out to be. But Coughlin has expressed dismay and anger at the ongoing problems that seem to be revealed by Lackland and other incidents. "[M]ilitary leadership, my chain of command and our government has failed me and countless others," she said in response to the Lackland allegations. "Since Tailhook we have seen repeated scandals, military leadership investigating itself, congressional hearings, reforms announced, training days ordered, laws passed," and yet harassment continues.[7] Coughlin concluded that an internal investigation by the Air Force was insufficient in the Lackland case. She pressed for congressional hearings and a chance for the victims to speak directly to lawmakers; without such steps, she feared, change would remain elusive.

At Issue: Sexual Assault and the Military looks at the issue of sexual harassment in the military and considers a number of important questions, including whether there is an epidemic of sexual violence in the military, what causes sexual violence in the military, and whether abuse and harassment should be handled through the chain of command or in civilian courts. The following viewpoints, in one way or another, examine whether the military has moved beyond Tailhook, and if not, how it can do so.

---

7. Quoted in Joyce Tsai, "Little Has Changed Since Tailhook, Based on Lackland Scandal Testimony," *Stars and Stripes*, January 23, 2013. http://www.stripes.com/little-has -changed-since-tailhook-based-on-lackland-scandal-testimony-1.205037.

1

Is Sexual Assault Really an "Epidemic"?

Rosa Brooks

Rosa Brooks is a law professor at Georgetown University and a Schwartz Senior Fellow at the New America Foundation. She served as a counselor to the US defense undersecretary for policy from 2009 to 2011 and previously served as a senior advisor at the US State Department.

The outcry over sexual assault in the military seems exaggerated. It is true that there is a problem with sexual assault in the military. However, rates of military sexual assault are actually lower than those in civilian groups, and lower than in colleges. The military needs to reduce sexual assaults, but the argument that sexual assault is particularly bad in the military is false. Instead, worries about sexual assault in the military may be linked to anxieties about women moving into combat positions and about allowing gays and lesbians to serve openly in the military.

*P*olitico calls it a "scandal," *Time* calls it an "epidemic," Defense Secretary Chuck Hagel describes it as a "scourge," and President Obama says it's "dangerous to our national security."

No, they're not talking about the spreading violence in Egypt, or hunger strikes at Guantanamo Bay, or even the high military suicide rate (we've already lost interest in that). The military crisis du jour—what Army Chief of Staff Ray Odierno calls the Army's "number one priority"—is sexual assault.

Sexual assault in the military is a genuine and serious problem, but the frantic rhetoric may be doing more harm than good. It conceals the progress the military has made in developing effective sexual assault prevention and response programs, and it distracts us from the even higher rates of sexual violence in comparable civilian populations. Ultimately, the current panic about sexual violence in the military may be less a reflection of sexual abuse trends than a reflection of broader societal anxieties about the changing role of women— and changing attitudes toward the age-old assumption that the military is synonymous with "manliness."

Sexual Assault in the Military

On the face of it, there's plenty of reason for the shock and outrage about sexual assault in the military. Extrapolating from responses to an anonymous survey of servicemembers, the Defense Department concluded that there may have been as many as 26,000 instances of "unwanted sexual contact" in 2012.

If you favor your glass half full, you might prefer to note that 93.9 percent of female servicemembers and 98.8 percent of male servicemembers had no unwanted sexual contact.

That's a whole lot of unwanted sexual contact—and whether it involves drunken groping or violent rape, sexual assaults can shatter careers and psyches. That's particularly true when the chain of command responds inappropriately, which still happens more often than it should. In the Pentagon's survey, some 67 percent of female servicemembers who said they experienced sexual assault never reported the assault to authorities—and of those "non-reporters," 66 percent said they felt "uncomfortable" reporting the incident, 51 percent lacked confidence that their report would be treated confidentially, and 47 percent said that fear of retaliation or reprisal prevented them from reporting the assaults.

There's no question that the military needs to do more to address the problem of sexual assault. Nevertheless, when you look more closely at the statistics, there's much less reason than commonly assumed to condemn the military. Although the *New York Times* editorial board insists that the military has an "entrenched culture of sexual violence," rates of sexual assault in the military in fact appear to be substantially lower than rates of sexual assault in comparable civilian populations. And although underreporting remains a serious problem, military personnel are substantially *more* likely than civilians to report sexual assaults to the authorities.

Relative to the size of the military population, 26,000 sexual assaults means that 6.1 percent of female servicemembers (and 1.2 percent of male servicemembers) experienced unwanted sexual contact during 2012. If you favor your glass half full, you might prefer to note that 93.9 percent of female servicemembers and 98.8 percent of male servicemembers had *no* unwanted sexual contact.

Not surprisingly, the Pentagon found that two-thirds of both the perpetrators and victims of reported sexual assaults were young—aged 24 or under. In part, this reflects the age distribution in the military as a whole (roughly half of all servicemembers are 17–24 years old), but it also reflects the fact that young people are disproportionately likely to engage in foolish and dangerous sexual behavior. They have less life and military experience than older servicemembers, less sexual experience, and less experience with the effects of alcohol, which is a factor in roughly half of military sexual assaults.

Sexual Assault Rates in Civilian Populations

To evaluate levels of sexual assault in the military, we need some points of comparison. First, consider sexual assault rates in the U.S. population as a whole. It's virtually impossible to get apples-to-apples comparisons, as various studies use slightly different definitions of sexual assault and look at different timeframes. But as Micah Zenko and Amelia Mae Wolff noted in a May 21 Foreign Policy article, the available evidence suggests that sexual assault rates in the civilian population are similar or higher than in the military. A 2010 study by the Centers for Disease Control (CDC) found that 18.3 percent of civilian women had been raped at some point in their lifetime, while 27.2 percent had experienced "unwanted sexual contact."

All in all, the rate of sexual assault in the military doesn't appear significantly higher than the rate in the broader civilian population.

In the 12 month period preceding the study, the CDC report found that 1.1 percent of women reported experiencing a rape or attempted rape, and an additional 5.6 percent of women reported some form of "other sexual violence," for an overall rape and sexual violence rate of 6.7 percent—slightly higher than the 6.1 percent of women reporting unwanted sexual contact in the 12 month period examined by the DOD study. And in the civilian population, as in the military, sexual assault rates are highest among the young: The CDC found that 79.6 percent of rape victims reported that they were first raped before they reached the age of 25.

It's also useful to examine sexual assault rates in another kind of institution populated mainly by 17- to 24-year-olds: the civilian university. Here again, direct comparisons are impossible due to variations in the available studies, but the evidence again suggests that sexual assault rates in the military are, if anything, lower than in similar civilian settings. One major study published by the Justice Department in 2000 found that 3.5 percent of college women reported a rape or attempted rape, while an additional 15.5 percent of college women reported that they had been "sexually victimized" in some other way during the academic year in which they were surveyed. Of these "non-rape" sexual victimizations, 7.7 percent involved physical force. Another 2007 Justice Department study found that "13.7 percent of undergraduate women had been victims of at least one completed sexual assault since entering college."

College women also appear to be even less likely than women in the military to report incidents of sexual assault to the authorities. Again, the caveat here is that the available studies looked at different time periods. But while 33 percent of female servicemembers who said they had experienced "unwanted sexual contact" in 2012 said they reported the assaults to military authorities, the Justice Department's 2000 study of sexual assaults on college campuses found that only *5 percent* of victims reported the incidents to college or law enforcement authorities. As with military women, the college women who did not report their experiences cited concerns about confidentiality, not being taken seriously, or being treated with hostility by the police.

The Military as Model?

Here's what it adds up to: All in all, the rate of sexual assault in the military doesn't appear significantly higher than the rate in the broader civilian population—and when you look at college campuses, which, like the military, are full of 17- to 24-year-olds, the military's sexual assault rates start looking low in comparison. The *New York Times* may be right to assert that the military has an "entrenched culture of sexual violence," but it would be more accurate to observe that the United States as a whole is characterized by an entrenched culture of sexual violence. Macho traditions notwithstanding, the military appears to have done a better job than most colleges of reducing the sexual assault rate and increasing women's willingness to report assaults to the authorities.

If military sexual assault rates are lower *than comparable civilian sexual assault rates, why all the frantic rhetoric recently about scandal, crisis, and epidemic?*

To be completely clear, this is not an argument for deciding that sexual assault isn't a problem in the military. Far from it: Sexual assaults continue to destroy too many lives and the high rates of military women who say they don't trust the system enough to report sexual assaults is evidence of the ongoing need to improve both prevention and response programs. Nevertheless, the military seems to be doing something right, since it has been able to bring sexual assault rates down below those prevalent in comparable civilian populations.

Even the best prevention programs are unlikely to eliminate *all* sexual crimes, but good programs taken seriously by committed leaders can make a real difference. The military should continue to study the factors that affect sexual assault rates and reporting rates, and continue to refine and improve prevention and response programs—and civilian universities seeking to lower their own sexual assault rates should consider looking to the military for examples and ideas.

Anxiety and Reaction: Changing Roles, Changing Norms

All this leaves something of a mystery. If military sexual assault rates are *lower* than comparable civilian sexual assault rates, why all the frantic rhetoric recently about scandal, crisis, and epidemic? Why isn't Congress saying, "Good job, DOD, you've demonstrated that a sustained focus on preventing sexual assault can keep military sexual assault rates below the rate in civilian populations. Now let's get that sexual assault rate down even further!"

Here's my theory.

The last two years have seen two policy changes that radically challenge traditional conceptions of masculinity and military ideals: the end of the ban on homosexuals serving openly in the military and the ban on women serving in combat positions. Change can feel threatening to those accustomed to the status quo, and social change this far-reaching has historically been accompanied by exaggerated claims of the harms likely to result. Sometimes these claims are well meaning; other times, not so much.

When President Harry Truman desegregated the U.S. military, critics warned that the move would lead to an increase in race-based tensions and violence. But as Truman and others had predicted, equality ultimately led to a decrease in incidents of discrimination and racial harassment, despite early hiccups. When ending "Don't Ask, Don't Tell" was debated, critics issued similar warnings about the impact of allowing gays and lesbians to serve openly. So far, the evidence suggests that this concern was just as unfounded.

Advocates for women in the military should press for additional sexual assault prevention reforms, but at the same time, they should insist that we keep the military's sexual assault rate in perspective.

When it comes to allowing women into the military, opponents have also asserted that allowing both sexes to serve side by side would lead to increasing sexual assaults against women—and any news of sexual assault in the military is used to justify opposition to full integration of women into the military. ("We told you so," crowed the right-wing Independent Women's Forum in response to a 2004 *Washington*

Post story on sexual assault in the Army, proudly noting its "long history" of warning that gender-integrated training would "inevitably" give rise to "sexual mishaps.")

Maybe it's just happenstance that the most recent round of hysteria about military sexual assault rates followed hard on the heels of the Pentagon's announcement that it would open all combat positions to women, but I doubt it.

Most of those speaking out against sexual violence in the military are strong supporters of the full integration of women into combat roles, but we should be aware that when remarks about "epidemics" and "crises" are carelessly made, they can discourage young women from pursuing military careers and play into the hands of those who would prefer to keep the "no girls allowed" sign on the door.

Advocates for women in the military should press for additional sexual assault prevention reforms, but at the same time, they should insist that we keep the military's sexual assault rate in perspective—and they should continue to point out how important and empowering it is for women to participate in the military alongside their male peers. A 2011 Pew survey found that post-9/11 female veterans were "just as likely as their male counterparts to say they have experienced the positive benefits of military service." Seventy-nine percent of women veterans believed their military service had "helped them get ahead in life," 87 percent said that serving in the military had built their self-confidence, and 93 percent felt the military had helped them "grow and mature as a person."

In the end, Gen. Martin Dempsey, the chairman of the Joint Chiefs of Staff, said it best: "We've had this ongoing issue with sexual harassment, sexual assault. . . . I believe it's because we've had separate classes of military personnel, at some level. Now, you know, it's far more complicated than that, but when you have one part of the population that is designated as warriors and another part that's designated as something else, I think that disparity begins to establish a psychology

17

that in some cases led to that environment. I have to believe, the more we can treat people equally, the more likely they are to treat each other equally."

Say it, brother.

2

Gen Helms and the Senator's "Hold"

James Taranto

James Taranto is a member of the Wall Street Journal *editorial board.*

The panic over military sexual assault threatens to criminalize male sexuality and deny crucial protections to the accused. This is illustrated in an incident where General Susan Helms granted clemency to a US Army captain accused of sexual assault. The assault charges were weak and uncorroborated; the captain was discharged from the Army but not listed as a sexual offender. This was a just outcome. Yet Missouri senator Claire McCaskill has taken action against Helms and prevented her from being promoted. This shows the irrationality and unjustness of the campaign against sexual assault, and it emphasizes again the importance of the clemency process.

Lt. Gen. Susan Helms is a pioneering woman who finds her career stalled because of a war on men—a political campaign against sexual assault in the military that shows signs of becoming an effort to criminalize male sexuality.

Gen. Helms is a 1980 graduate of the Air Force Academy who became an astronaut in 1990. She was a crewman on four space-shuttle missions and a passenger on two, traveling to the International Space Station and back 5 ½ months later. Two days after arriving at the station in 2001, she, along with fellow astronaut Jim Voss, conducted history's longest space-walk—8 hours, 56 minutes—to work on a docking device.

In March, President Obama nominated Gen. Helms to serve as vice commander of the Air Force Space Command. But Sen. Claire McCaskill, a Missouri Democrat who sits on the Armed Services Committee, has placed a "permanent hold" on the nomination.

At issue is the general's decision in February 2012 to grant clemency to an officer under her command. Capt. Matthew Herrera had been convicted by a court-martial of aggravated sexual assault. Ms. McCaskill said earlier this month that the clemency decision "sent a damaging message to survivors of sexual assault who are seeking justice in the military justice system."

Gen. Helms concluded that the defendant was a more reliable witness than the accuser, and that prosecutors had failed to prove beyond a reasonable doubt that Capt. Herrera did not reasonably believe the accuser had consented.

To describe the accuser in the Herrera case as a "survivor" is more than a little histrionic. The trial was a he-said/she-said dispute between Capt. Herrera and a female second lieutenant about a drunken October 2009 sexual advance in the back seat of a moving car. The accuser testified that she fell asleep, then awoke to find her pants undone and Capt. Herrera touching her genitals. He testified that she was awake, undid her own pants, and responded to his touching by resting her head on his shoulder.

Two other officers were present—the designated driver and a front-seat passenger, both lieutenants—but neither noticed the hanky-panky. Thus on the central questions of initiation and consent, it was her word against his.

On several other disputed points, however, the driver, Lt. Michelle Dickinson, corroborated Capt. Herrera's testimony and contradicted his accuser's.

Capt. Herrera testified that he and the accuser had flirted earlier in the evening; she denied it. Lt. Dickinson agreed with him. The accuser testified that she had told Lt. Dickinson before getting into the car that she found Capt. Herrera "kind of creepy" and didn't want to share the back seat with him; Lt. Dickinson testified that she had said no such thing. And the accuser denied ever resting her head on Capt. Herrera's shoulder (although she acknowledged putting it in his lap). Lt. Dickinson testified that at one point during the trip, she looked back and saw the accuser asleep with her head on Capt. Herrera's shoulder.

In addition, the accuser exchanged text messages with Capt. Herrera after the incident. She initially claimed to have done so only a "couple times" but changed her testimony after logs of the text traffic revealed there were 116 messages, 51 of them sent by her.

The presumption that reckless men are criminals while reckless women are victims makes a mockery of any notion that the sexes are equal.

Based on all this, Gen. Helms concluded that the defendant was a more reliable witness than the accuser, and that prosecutors had failed to prove beyond a reasonable doubt that Capt. Herrera did not reasonably believe the accuser had consented. He did not escape punishment: Gen. Helms accepted a reduced plea of guilty to an "indecent act." Capt. Herrera was thereby spared the lifelong stigma of being listed on a sex-offender registry—but not of involuntary discharge from the service, which took effect in December.

"Immediately after this incident, there was no indication by any party that a sexual assault had taken place," Gen. Helms wrote in a Feb. 24, 2012, memo explaining her decision. "The time delay between the event and the court-martial was approximately two years, and none of the witnesses, including the accused and the [alleged] victim, knew for at least a year that a court-martial would be convened for it."

In the interim, another servicewoman, Staff Sgt. Jennifer Robinson, had come forward to accuse Capt. Herrera of sexual assault. In her case, the incident had occurred in his bedroom, where she voluntarily accompanied him. The court-martial acquitted him of that charge on the ground that she had consented. (Sgt. Robinson, who has since been promoted to technical sergeant, revealed her identity in a March interview with the Air Force Times.)

It's fair to say that Capt. Herrera seems to have a tendency toward sexual recklessness. Perhaps that makes him unsuitable to serve as an officer in the U.S. Air Force. But his accusers acted recklessly too. The presumption that reckless men are criminals while reckless women are victims makes a mockery of any notion that the sexes are equal.

More important, Sen. McCaskill's blocking of Gen. Helms's nomination makes a mockery of basic principles of justice. As the general observed in her memo: "Capt Herrera's conviction should not rest on [the accuser's] view of her victimization, but on the law and convincing evidence, consistent with the standards afforded any American who finds him/herself on trial for a crime of this severity."

On Friday the House passed a defense bill that would strip commanders of the authority to grant clemency. That would be a mistake. The Herrera case demonstrates that the authority offers crucial protection for the accused.

Military officers and lawmakers alike swear an oath to "support and defend the Constitution of the United States." In the case of Matthew Herrera, Gen. Helms lived up to that commitment. Will Sen. McCaskill?

3

Sexual Assault Is a Long-Term Problem in the Military

Zoë Carpenter

Zoë Carpenter is a reporter in the Washington, DC bureau of The Nation. *She has written for* Rolling Stone, Guernica, *and the* Poughkeepsie Journal.

Brenda Hoster, a sergeant major in the US Army, accused her boss Gene C. McKinney of sexually assaulting her in a hotel room in 1996. She spoke out against the assault, but the Army did not convict McKinney, and Hoster retired from the military two years later. She spoke out again when McKinney was appointed to a panel to investigate sexual assault. Hoster says that the military has moved slowly or not at all in confronting sexual assault, and she expresses anger that her own experiences have not spurred more change.

When Brenda Hoster publicly accused the sergeant major of the Army of sexually assaulting her, it nearly destroyed her life. She thought it would be worth it.

"I felt like what I did was the right thing, the ethical thing, not just for me but for all military men and women," Hoster, a retired sergeant major and public affairs specialist, said in one of two phone conversations. Her complaints against the Army's top enlisted soldier were part of a wave of sex scandals that rocked the military in the 1990s. Today, Congress is still debating how to best reform the military justice system.

"Nothing's changed. Why is that?" asked Hoster. "I feel like my journey was for nothing."

It's been nearly two decades since Hoster spoke out against Sergeant Major Gene McKinney, who was her boss. She'd stayed quiet for months after the alleged assault, which she said occurred in a Honolulu hotel room in 1996. Hoster said her superiors at the Pentagon told her to resolve her issues with McKinney (who was later acquitted) on her own, and later refused her requests to transfer. Feeling powerless and alone, Hoster chose to end her twenty-two-year career. "There was very little confidence back then about being a whistle-blower," she said. "It was fight or flight, and I flew."

Around the same time a sex scandal at an Army training base in Aberdeen, Maryland, in which twelve officers were accused of assaulting female trainees, sparked public concern about assault in the military. Aberdeen came on the heels of the 1991 Navy Tailhook scandal, in which more than 100 officers were accused of assault or harassment. In response to the Aberdeen incident, the Army commissioned a panel to investigate its sexual harassment policies.

Victims' advocates, veterans and some active duty officers argue that forcing victims to report to commanders exposes them to conflicts of interest and retaliation.

One of the appointees was McKinney. "I said, 'Oh, *hell* no,'" remembered Hoster. In February of 1997 she decided to go public and filed a formal complaint with the Army. Five other women came forward to accuse McKinney for separate incidents. "It was about the ethics of it—nobody would do anything to help me, and now this guy was going to be on this panel investigating sexual harassment. To me, it was like nobody cared. I cared, and I spoke. And I paid dearly for it," said Hoster.

After decades of scandals, investigatory panels and trials, the military still has not stemmed the sexual assault epidemic. Nor has it found a way to assure service members like Hoster that they will be heard and protected if they report crimes against them. Only two in ten service members who suffered "unwanted sexual contact" in 2012 reported the incidents. As the system is set up now they must do so through their commanding officer, who then decides whether the accusations warrant a trial by court martial.

"I think nothing's changed because of the way that these things are brought to justice—or not to justice. I think a lot of it has to do with antiquated, non-functioning military justice system," Hoster said.

Congress reached a similar conclusion last year after a series of hearings, and passed a number of reforms to the military justice system along with the annual defense spending bill. The new legislation bars commanders from overturning jury convictions, criminalizes retaliation against people who report sexual assault, mandates dishonorable discharge for anyone convicted of sex crimes, and removes the statute of limitations for such cases.

But Congress has not yet voted on the most significant and controversial reform proposed—Senator Kirsten Gillibrand's Military Justice Improvement Act, which would put military lawyers, rather than commanding officers, in charge of sexual assault prosecutions. Victims' advocates, veterans and some active duty officers argue that forcing victims to report to commanders exposes them to conflicts of interest and retaliation, and disadvantages accused and accuser alike by putting legal decisions in the hands of officers without legal training. Fifty-four senators—including nine Republicans—support Gillibrand's bill, which the chamber will take up some time in March [2014]. The military's top brass and two key Democrats on the Armed Services Committee, chairman Carl Levin and Claire McCaskill, oppose the measure, saying it would undermine commanders' ability to enforce order and discipline in the ranks.

"From my experience, victims—and I hate that word, but can't think of anything else—the victims don't have someone they can trust to go to," Hoster said. "How the hell would they have confidence in the chain of command right now? How could anyone have confidence, with all this stuff happening for years?"

In 1997, after what Hoster described as a "nasty" trial, McKinney was acquitted of all but one count of obstructing justice. Hoster struggled to keep her life together in El Paso, Texas, where she lived "like a recluse." She had devoted her life to the Army: it gave her a ticket out of small-town Pennsylvania, and she loved the culture of discipline. Without it, she drifted. It took about ten years for the alienation and defensiveness to fade. Now she works for the Veterans Administration in San Antonio, which she considers an extension of her service in the Army. She describes her life largely in positive terms, but acknowledged that occasionally something rekindles her memory of the assault and its drawn-out aftermath.

"I am a lot better after all these years, but when I start talking about it . . ." Hoster began to cry, softly. "It never goes away. You just need to learn how to deal with it better. It will always feel bad."

What makes Hoster angry now is not what she says happened to her; it's that speaking out didn't make more of a difference for others in the military. In her work Hoster frequently encounters other veterans struggling with military sexual trauma. "It just disgusts me that it's still happening," Hoster said.

Gillibrand's bill is likely to draw a filibuster, and both sides are contending for a handful of undecided votes. Opponents say the reforms that passed in December are sufficient correctives, and they should be given time to work before imposing deeper change.

Hoster is tired of the military asking for more time. "I fell on my sword for something back then," she said when asked why the debate still mattered to her. "I'm not gonna turn my back on it."

4

Reports Show Sexual Assault in the Military Is Skyrocketing

Robert C. Koehler

Robert C. Koehler is an award-winning, Chicago-based journalist and nationally syndicated writer. He is the author of Courage Grows Strong at the Wound.

The number of sexual assaults in the military is rising. Meanwhile, the military establishment is unwilling to allow a civilian body to evaluate sexual assault claims, a small and obvious first step toward addressing the crisis. The problem may be that the military's culture of dominance is ill-suited to address these issues. The sexual assault problem in the military, therefore, is structural and ideological and will be very difficult to change.

Maybe the problem is that rape is an extension of military culture. And it's metastasizing, even as legislation to address it stays trapped in congressional subcommittee.

Numbers Rising

Scandals and outrage come and go, but rape is ever-present. In 2011, a Pentagon report estimated that 19,000 sexual assaults had occurred in the U.S. military, of which barely 3,000 were reported because of the stigma and risk involved in doing so. The "I own you" system of military justice traditionally turns on the victim far more than the accused. That year, in response to the shocking statistics, U.S. Rep. Jackie Speier (D-Calif.) introduced a bill that would, among other things, remove the investigation of rape cases from the military chain of command, which has far more interest in ignoring the problem than prosecuting it.

Now a new Pentagon report is out, estimating that 26,000 cases of sexual assault occurred in the U.S. military in 2012, with, once again, just over 3,000 incidents reported. And Speier's legislation has been sitting the whole time in the House Armed Services Committee, denied even a hearing.

"The military doesn't want this and the committee tends to be very deferential to what the military wants," Speier told Northern California public TV station KQED. "This is one of those issues where what the military wants is not good enough for all the men and women in the military who want to serve without being jumped by a sexual predator in the night."

Note that Speier's legislation is several steps removed from actually identifying and eliminating the root causes of military rape—which Michigan Sen. Carl Levin, chairman of the Senate Committee on Armed Services, called a "plague" that needs to be addressed "swiftly and decisively." Speier's bill would simply allow victims to report the crime in relative safety, a fairly basic precondition for after-the-fact justice.

In 2011, the Pentagon's own estimate put the number of sexual assaults that year at 19,000. In 2012, it rose to 26,000.

The current system puts investigation and prosecution into the hands of commanding officers, who often enough have a powerful interest in maintaining the façade that everything is fine; and women and men who have the audacity to report sexual assault muddy that façade, often putting their own careers in jeopardy. Away from the spotlight of public scandal, those in power have no interest in changing the system.

But sexual assault scandals don't go away. So far this month, three military officers tasked with sexual assault prevention—at the Army's Fort Campbell, Ky., and Fort Hood, Texas, along with the leader of the Air Force's branch of the Sexual Assault Prevention and Response Program—have themselves been arrested for sexual misconduct or stalking. Their arrests, combined with the release of the Pentagon's report indicating an enormous rise in what, a year previously, had already been a shockingly high estimate of sexual assault occurrences in the military, has once again triggered public and political outrage.

A Structural Problem

I repeat: In 2011, the Pentagon's own estimate put the number of sexual assaults that year at 19,000. In 2012, it rose to 26,000.

Taking the rape reporting process out of the chain of command and creating an investigative office outside the Defense Department, while no doubt a good idea, strikes me as being an inadequate response to the phenomenon. That even such a relatively minor, reasonable change is, apparently, impossible to accomplish gives it a certain cachet in the discussion. It's the idea that politicians and the media have focused on for two successive scandal cycles, keeping the discussion from becoming a deeper look at the root causes.

Sen. Kirsten Gillibrand (D-NY) did tell MSNBC that a policy of zero tolerance toward rape isn't good enough. What we need, she said, is "zero occurrence." Amen, senator, but what are the steps we must take to bring this about?

Like suicide, sexual assault is skyrocketing in the military. Why? Could it be that the problem is deeply structural? Could it be that it's related to the domination culture the military embodies, not to mention the brutally immoral, pointless wars we've been waging for the past decade-plus? Could it have something to do with the idea that what goes around comes around?

In 2011, after the earlier scandal, when Speier first proposed her legislation, I wrote: "Maybe it's time to look at the values themselves—beginning with those of our military culture, which is the model, and indeed the metaphor, for every other form of domination culture: The prime value is winning, achieving dominance over some sort of enemy or 'other.' Around this core of dominance, we construct a fortress of honor, righteousness, cleanliness of mind and spirit. We revere the fortress, but in its dark interior, our natural impulses are ungoverned and often manifest themselves in perverse mockery of the values we salute."

In a culture based on winning, the rapist is the "winner." Maybe that's the problem. And it permeates not just personal behavior but national policy.

5

Naval Academy Says Increase in Sex Assault Reports Shows Progress

Matthew Hay Brown

Matthew Hay Brown is the politics and government editor at The Baltimore Sun.

The Naval Academy has had an increase in the number of reports of sexual assault, which shows that there is more willingness to report these incidents to authorities. This is a positive development. The Naval Academy has also worked to teach students about sexual assault, and has especially worked with student athletes. The Academy is committed to eliminating sexual assault and confronting the problem of sexual misconduct on campus.

Naval Academy officials say an increase in reports of sexual assault shows they are making progress against the crime.

Fifteen sexual assaults were reported at the academy during the 2012–2013 academic year, the Pentagon said Friday, up from 13 the year before.

The data came in the Pentagon's Annual Report on Sexual Harassment and Violence at the Military Service Academies. Reports of sexual assault fell at the U.S. Military Academy and the U.S. Air Force Academy, for an overall drop across the academies from 80 in 2011–2012 to 70 in 2012–2013.

Maj. Gen. Jeffrey Snow, head of the Pentagon's Sexual Assault Prevention and Response Office, said it was not possible to say whether the decline in reports indicates a decline in assaults. He said the office would survey cadets and midshipmen this year to gain a better understanding of the number of assaults taking place.

"I want to make one thing clear," Snow told reporters Friday. "Sexual assault is a crime and has no place at the academies, just as it has no place in the armed forces."

Past surveys have indicated that hundreds of cadets and midshipman are subjected to unwanted sexual contact each year.

During their four years on campus ... midshipmen receive more than 30 hours of [sexual assault prevention] training and education—more than at any other college or university in the country.

The drop in reports at the academies runs counter to the recent militarywide trend of increased reporting—a trend that officials have said indicates a growing trust in the military justice system.

Nancy J. Parrish, president of the victim advocacy group Protect Our Defenders, expressed concern. "That number is going in the wrong direction," she said.

At the Naval Academy, eight of the 15 reports involved an alleged attack by one midshipman on another. The rest either predated the alleged victim's arrival at the academy or were perpetrated by someone other than a midshipman.

Cmdr. John Schofield, an academy spokesman, said the year-over-year increase in reports "indicates that we are successfully cultivating a climate where victims feel safe reporting assaults."

The authors of the report released Friday conclude that leaders, faculty and staff at the academies are committed to eliminating sexual assault, and the "vast majority" of students "generally support the values of mutual respect and dignity."

"However, the extent to which cadets and midshipmen feel free to act on these values varies. . . . At each of the three academies, there is evidence that some cadets and midshipmen disregarded academy policies and practices in these areas."

The authors cite as an example the midshipmen who rented an off-campus house in Annapolis, in violation of academy rules, and hosted parties at which alcohol was served to minors.

The house on Witmer Court is where three members of Navy's football team were alleged to have sexually assaulted a female midshipman in April 2012. One midshipman faces a court-martial in that incident. Academy Superintendent Vice Adm. Michael H. Miller decided not to pursue charges against another, and charges against a third were dismissed Friday.

Schofield said midshipmen are briefed by the sexual assault prevention and response staff on their first day on campus. During their four years on campus, the academy spokesman said, midshipmen receive more than 30 hours of such mandatory training and education—more than at any other college or university in the country.

He said special effort is focused on academy athletes. He said all sports team captains, company commanders and brigade leaders participated in a leadership retreat last summer at which sexual harassment and assault was a central theme.

All varsity athletes are required to sign a code of conduct at the beginning of the year that addresses sexual harassment and sexual assault, Schofield said, and the academy superintendent met with each varsity team and coach during the summer and fall to "reinforce expectations."

Schofield said athletic association employees met with the academy sexual assault prevention and response staff and attended training sessions. "The Naval Academy continues to promote a positive command climate where incidents of sexual harassment and sexual assault are immediately identified and ultimately eliminated," he said. "As an institution producing future leaders for the Navy and Marine Corps, nothing is more important than instilling and maintaining a climate where all midshipmen always treat one another—and expect to be treated—with dignity and mutual respect." The authors of the report write that the Naval Academy "demonstrated a commitment to increasing awareness of sexual assaults and harassment at the academy, developing and conducting high quality training, and improving the victim experience."

They encouraged officials to continue to incorporate "sexual assault prevention learning objectives" in academic curriculum and to develop measures to judge effectiveness and prevention.

6

Porn Consumption Contributes to Sexual Assault in the Military

Peter J. Smyczek and Kenneth Artz

Peter J. Smyczek is a first lieutenant in the US Air Force Reserves and is attached as an IMA (part-time reservist) to the 42nd ABW Legal Office, Maxwell Air Force Base, in Alabama. As a civilian, he serves as a prosecutor with the attorney general's office for the state of Alabama. Kenneth Artz is an active duty major in the US Air Force and member of the US Air Force JAG Corps; he also formerly served as an Air Force Strategic Policy Fellow in Washington, DC.

Pornography is dangerously addictive, and many studies have linked porn consumption to sex crimes and violence. It is reasonable to conclude, therefore, that the high levels of sexual assault in the military are linked to the high levels of porn consumption among military personnel. The military should work to reduce porn consumption. It should warn personnel about the dangers of porn addiction and the link between porn and violence.

It is bad enough when high-ranking military officers are arrested for sexual assault, including instructors who have assaulted trainees. It is almost unthinkable that two military members recently arrested happened to be in charge of or were associated with sexual assault prevention programs for their respective services. It is not hyperbole to say that the US military is in a sexual assault crisis not seen since the Navy's Tailhook scandal [in 1991, when dozens of people were allegedly sexually assaulted].

To extract itself from this sexual assault wash cycle, the Air Force, in which we serve, along with other branches of the military, must take swift action to recognize many of the underlying behaviors that lead to sexual assault and warn its Airmen accordingly. Specifically, it is imperative that the Air Force recognize the direct link between sexual assaults and the elevated amount of pornography consumption in its ranks. Pornography has become the new drug of many Airmen, and the service must help its members deal with this addictive new health hazard.

Regrettably, the Air Force is still not warning its Airmen of the dangers to their lives and careers associated with frequent consumption of legal adult pornography.

Porn Addiction

Members of the Judge Advocate General's Corps (JAGs) can help solve this problem and provide insight from their unique perspective on military duty. Military legal offices work closely with the military commanders to help maintain good order and discipline, and as a result, get to see the "ugly side" of the military services. Daily, they conduct investigations of and prosecute crimes committed by military members. JAGs also provide free legal advice to service members on a whole range of issues such as divorce, which offers JAGs another window into the causes of common personal problems. Many JAGs also gain rare insight into the root causes of crimes like sexual assault committed by Airmen.

The military's sexual assault problem is grim, but unfortunately, the current Air Force sexual assault prevention training, although well-intended, is not cutting the mustard. A brief anecdote might help illuminate the issue.

The thermonuclear missile base, Francis E. Warren Air Force Base, is located on the windswept grassy plains of eastern Wyoming. A few years back, the base was struck by a rash of child pornography cases among its ranks. Numerous Airmen were prosecuted for possession of child pornography after local authorities discovered that they had downloaded images and videos from file sharing websites. The legal office spent years prosecuting these tragic cases.

To stop the bleeding, JAGs fanned out across the base to warn Airmen about how to avoid child pornography. For the most part, the JAGs simply advised them to be cautious in which websites they visit.

Tragically, they often failed to advise them to stay away from the highly addictive, legal, adult online pornography, which in nearly every case preceded the descent into the seedy world of child pornography. Unsurprisingly, child pornography crime still occurs at F. E. Warren and many other bases. Regrettably, the Air Force is still not warning its Airmen of the dangers to their lives and careers associated with frequent consumption of legal adult pornography.

Better training is needed now more than ever because the military's sexual assault problem is grim. According to a recent Department of Defense study, 26,000 military members reported being a victim of some type of sexual assault last year. This number is up from 19,300 reports in 2010. The sexual assault statistics in the Air Force alone are no better. The preliminary figures for 2012 reveal almost 800 reported cases, which is a 30 percent increase. The Pentagon recently admitted that sexual assault within the military is a "persistent problem," and that the services need to do more to prevent them.

Work to Change People

Current sexual assault prevention training can best be described as changing conditions without changing people. This is a recipe for failure. A 2012 Joint Chiefs of Staff Strategic Direction letter on sexual assault prevention and response confirmed that the current training falls short of being effective and stressed that reducing high-risk behaviors and personal vulnerabilities associated with sexual assault must become part of the training. Current Air Force training does not address these types of behaviors and root causes, such as pornography consumption, that lead to sex crimes.

One out of ten in the general civilian population is addicted to internet pornography. Pornographic consumption and addiction are believed to be much higher in the military, though, because of the largely young male population and frequent deployments.

In fact, in an interview with the *Army Times*, Navy Lt. Michael Howard, a licensed therapist and military chaplain, believes that at least 20 percent of the military is addicted to online pornography. The common theme among many military chaplains is that addiction to internet pornography is one of the biggest, if not the biggest, personal problem facing our military members today.

In August 2012, the chief of the Defense Missile Agency was forced to issue a warning to its employees to stop accessing pornographic images from their government computers.

It is not uncommon for military members to come home from a deployment addicted to pornography. Military spouses often complain about these devastating addictions post-deployment.

The military's pornography problem continually grabs news headlines. An Army Colonel stationed at the Army War

College in Pennsylvania was recently arrested for possessing more than 10,000 images of suspected child pornography on his personal laptop. In 2006, seven paratroopers from the famed 82nd Airborne Division stationed at Fort Bragg, North Carolina, were caught appearing on a gay pornographic website.

In August 2012, the chief of the Defense Missile Agency was forced to issue a warning to its employees to stop accessing pornographic images from their government computers and to stop sending pornography through their network e-mails.

The Chief of Staff of the Air Force, General Mark Welsh, recognized this pornography problem and recently ordered all Air Force bases to remove all sexually explicit images from work areas. Countless pornographic images were found and removed. In addition, the Secretary of Defense, Chuck Hagel, recently ordered a similar inspection to be conducted at all military bases.

Linked to Sex Crimes

Although it is an issue that some still try to debate, mounting research shows that legal adult pornography is dangerous, especially the highly addictive internet pornography available at all times and on nearly every communication device. Research also shows a direct link between pornography consumption and the commission of sex crimes. In fact, in a recent interview, General Welsh alluded to the link between pornographic images adorning walls and a culture of sexual assault.

Like many JAGs, civilian prosecutors have also learned from their cases that pornography consumption can create and feed deviant and dangerous behaviors. The infamous serial killer Ted Bundy, who raped and killed thirty-six to fifty young women and girls, placed much of the blame for his actions on pornography just before he was executed in 1989, saying:

In the beginning, it [pornography] fuels this kind of thought process. ... Like an addiction, you keep craving something that is harder, harder, something which gives you a greater sense of excitement—until you reach a point where the pornography only goes so far, you reach that jumping-off point where you begin to wonder if maybe actually doing it would give you that which is beyond just reading or looking at it.

Another infamous serial killer, Arthur Gary Bishop, who was executed in 1983 for sodomizing and killing five young boys, stated that "pornography was not the only negative influence in my life, but its effect on me was devastating ... pornography was a determining factor in my downfall."

As with drug users, those who use pornography seek more and more deviant materials to maintain their previous level of sexual arousal.

Further, many years before the creation of the Internet, J. Edgar Hoover, former director of the FBI, described pornography's influence on sex crimes: "What we do know is that an overwhelmingly large number of cases of sex crimes is associated with pornography. We know that sex criminals read it and are clearly influenced by it. ... I believe pornography is a major source of sex violence. ..."

Pornography is effective at shaping both beliefs and behaviors about sex. Pornography poses such a danger not only because it assaults a human being's emotional psyche, but also because it causes physical addictions similar to hard drugs. Consequently, research shows that most people who commit a sex crime regularly view pornography.

According to Robert Weiss, director of the Sexual Recovery Institute in Los Angeles, "Online porn is to sex addiction what crack cocaine is to drug addiction." As detailed in the *Army Times*, a brain scan of a sex addict looks the same as the scan of someone who has just used cocaine. As the brain receives the pornographic images it releases adrenaline into the bloodstream, increasing the heart rate and causing sweaty palms and dilation of the eyes. The pituitary gland and hypothalamus secrete endorphins to produce dopamine, which opens up the pleasure centers of the brain; and too much dopamine is what actually causes the addiction.

Several studies have shown that all persons, normal and unbalanced, who view pornography develop a craving for more deviant materials. Many persons even begin to employ more violent methods in their sexual relations. As with drug users, those who use pornography seek more and more deviant materials to maintain their previous level of sexual arousal.

In 1988, the FBI reported that 81 percent of violent sexual offenders regularly read or viewed violent pornography. A twenty-year FBI study indicates that 81 percent of sex murderers name pornography as their most significant sexual interest, and police investigators routinely find porn in the homes of sex-crime suspects.

Limit Pornography, Reduce Assaults

The research detailed above is just the tip of the iceberg documenting the connection between pornography consumption and sex crimes (websites www.pornharms.com and www .fightthenewdrug.com contain a plethora of additional research). Academic research and the documented evidence of law enforcement officials leave little doubt that pornography consumption is a significant motivator of sex crimes. It only makes sense then, that to reduce sexual assaults, the Air Force must work to limit or prevent the consumption of pornography.

Many may scoff at such an approach. They may believe pornography is victimless and in fact can be healthy for their sex lives, or even serve as a cure for loneliness while being away from one's family. Others may not be convinced of the connection between pornography and deviant behavior because they themselves consume pornography and have no desire to commit a sex crime.

But it would be foolish to ignore the well-documented risks associated with pornography consumption. As with any other highly addictive substance, the prudent course would be to warn our military members about these risks. The military, serving the paternal role it does, already deals with alcohol and narcotic consumption in similar and ordered fashion. Leadership should also take action to help those already addicted to pornography before their lives or careers (or the lives of others) are ruined by this addiction. The Air Force specifically already has many resources in place at the base clinic, base chaplaincy, and base legal offices, among other places, to help Airmen escape pornography addiction. Additional training for commanders would be in order to educate them on this problem so they can engage with their units.

The time is now to begin this anti-pornography training campaign before more of our heroes are lost to this dangerous drug.

Disclaimer: The Authors have no intention of promulgating Department of Defense or Department of the Air Force policy. The opinions and conclusions expressed in this publication are solely those of the authors and do not necessarily reflect the opinion of The Judge Advocate General, The Judge Advocate General's Corps, the State of Alabama, or any other department or agency of the US Government.

7

Not Porn but Wars Have Triggered the Rise in Military Sexual Assault

Ana Marie Cox

Ana Marie Cox is a political columnist for the Guardian *newspaper in the United States and the founding editor of the blog Wonkette.*

Senators have argued that the cause of sexual assault in the military is porn or hormones or more women in the service. However, men themselves experience sexual assault in the military, suggesting that simplistic explanations are not sufficient. Instead, it seems possible that elevated sexual violence is the result of increased stress among the troops caused by the nature of modern warfare and the increasing length of deployments.

The Senate hearings held last week on sexual assault in the military were laughable. "Laughable" in the sense that some of the statements made by those senators were shockingly sexist and mind-bogglingly inappropriate.

Not Porn, Not Hormones

Jeff Sessions of Alabama blamed pornography, specifically, and "a culture awash in sexual activity," for the high number of assaults. Georgia's Saxby Chambliss suggested, with appropriately naïve exclamation, that it's not nurture but nature that's the problem:

"Gee whiz, the hormone level created by nature sets in place the possibility for these types of things to occur."

Not only is their science iffy, but their logic also fails on its surface. Pornography exists outside military bases, and surely there are hormones awash in the culture at large. So, are the alarming increases in sexual assaults, you know, everywhere else? As a matter of fact, instances of rape and sexual assault against women have been on a steady decline (dropping 58% between 1995 and 2010), despite increases in the *reporting* of such crimes. The only place sexual assault has seen a dramatic rise is in the military.

The data extrapolated from a survey of those who experienced sexual assault (whether it was reported or not) indicated that men were the victims of assault even more often than women.

To be fair, women are joining the military more often than they used to: they make up 14% of enlisted soldiers (up from 2% in 1973) and 16% of officers (up from 4%). John McCain appeared to argue that maybe this was the problem, and indicated that the solution would be to warn women away from service:

"Just last night, a woman came to me and said her daughter wanted to join the military and could I give my unqualified support for her doing so."

At the time, I mocked McCain for his hesitancy; by his logic, an even better solution to the problem of sexual assault would be a military made up of *only* women. Or perhaps he should discourage men from joining as well: for sure we would solve the problem of sexual assault in the military if there were no military at all.

But McCain's full remarks actually hint that he's given the issue more thought than his colleagues:

"At its core, this is an issue about defending basic human rights but it's also a long-term threat to the strength of our military. We have to ask ourselves: if left uncorrected, what impact will this problem have on recruitment and retention of qualified men and women?"

Men Are Victims

McCain's thinking is often pretty inscrutable—it's the maverickiness—so I can't say for sure if he's onto what I think he's onto, but as far as I can tell, McCain was the only member of the armed forces committee to even suggest that sexual assault is a problem for men in the military as well as women. And not just in the "it looks bad"/honor/integrity sense: the Department of Defense report that spurred such outrage (and the hearing) found that 12% of those who *reported* sexual assault were men.

What's more, the data extrapolated from a survey of those who experienced sexual assault (whether it was reported or not) indicated that men were the victims of assault even more often than women. Indeed, if the survey data is truly reflective of reality, men are the victims of *a majority* of sexual assaults in the military: an estimated 14,000 men, as opposed to 12,000 women. (Since there are so many more men than women overall, the percentages of sexual assault victims among all male and female soldiers look more like what you'd expect: 6.1% of female soldiers, and 1.2% of the men.)

Still, the staggering number of sexual assaults on men—and 98% of them are committed by other men—puts to lie the chauvinistic fantasies of Sessions and Chambliss. I guess, though, if you really believe sexual violence is caused by "hormones" and out-of-control lust, then maybe you'd also concede that sex-crazed young men aren't picky about the gender of their victims. I don't think that's the case, however. I think these numbers suggest something darker about the already-disturbing data: that there's not something about women's presence in the military that leads to high rates of sexual assault; it's something about *being in the military*.

I should clarify: it's something about being in the military *today*, at this moment in history, fighting the kinds of wars we're fighting with the kinds of troops we have. Most of my immediate family has served at one point or another, and I generally hold the view that those drawn to fight for our country are more honorable than the public at large and hold themselves to a higher standard of personal behavior. That's part of what makes the report so chilling—these people are the best of what our country has to offer, and they are subject to (and signed up for) a level of discipline that most of us don't want and couldn't stomach. So, what explains the horrific behavior among those who are in general exemplary citizens? Is it just a failure to screen against predators?

Troops serve longer and more numerous tours, and function for longer periods under tangential supervision. There's a clear psychic toll.

The brass questioned last week admitted that's a possibility. Under questioning from McCain, General Jack Dempsey, the chairman of the Joint Chiefs of Staff, admitted there are "inadequate protections for precluding that from happening, so a sex offender could, in fact, find their way into the armed forces of the United States."

Too Much War

Personally, in looking for answers to this menace, I can't help but notice the other set of statistics that illustrates a form of corrosion among those who aim to be invincible: the growing number of soldiers and veterans diagnosed with mental illnesses and chemical dependency. In the past 12 years, the number of suicides among active-duty troops has reached record levels: last year, more died by their own hand than by enemy fire. The two epidemics are equally embarrassing to military leaders, perhaps there's a further connection, as well.

In discussing the problem of suicides and depression, some analysts have wondered about the role played by the tactics of modern warfare: it is more random, more prolonged, "asymmetric," and, as we have been reminded this week, fraught with confusion about who the enemy is. Troops serve longer and more numerous tours, and function for longer periods under tangential supervision. There's a clear psychic toll.

It's a truism among feminists—if not senators—that rape is a crime of violence, not of sexual attraction. It's a function of rage, not lust. Could it be that the real crisis in today's military is tied to not who these soldiers are, but the nature of what we're asking them to do?

8

Sexual Harassment in the Military: What Female Cadets Have to Say

Anna Mulrine

Anna Mulrine is a staff writer for the Christian Science Monitor.

A survey of students at the military service academies revealed that sexual harassment and sexist comments are very common. This is especially disturbing, since harassment is correlated with sexual assault and sexual violence. Women students at the academies said that harassment and sexism were especially difficult to deal with because of the low number of women in the academies. They also said that different physical standards for women, and the fact that women are restricted from certain combat roles, adds to a culture of resentment toward and prejudice against women.

A new Pentagon report offers a fascinating window into how students at the service academies feel the military should best handle sexual harassment and assault on campus—and why they occur.

Harassment Leads to Assault

These insights are gleaned from verbatim comments shared in focus groups conducted by Pentagon officials. They're in an appendix to the report, released Friday, that shows that incidents of sexual assault at two of America's three service academies are down. But there are no data to indicate whether the downtick "is due to fewer assaults occurring or due to fewer victims opting to report," said Maj. Gen. Jeffrey Snow, director of the Defense Department's Sexual Assault Prevention and Response Office (SAPRO).

The Pentagon watches the results of this congressionally mandated report closely, since "the academy is where we develop future leaders of the military," Snow noted during a briefing with reporters Friday.

Another key finding in the report: Cadets at the academies often say that peer pressure is a "barrier to reporting," Snow said. "That's not good."

The study also found that "the rates for crude and offensive behavior—this is your typical locker room talk—and for sexist behavior on the 2012 survey—those were high," said Elizabeth Van Winkle, deputy branch chief of the Defense Manpower Data Center, which conducted the focus groups with students at the academies.

Between 80 and 90 percent of women indicated that they had been the object of sexist comments in the past 12 months. Defense officials sought to bore into those figures to see if they were really accurate.

There is a strong positive correlation between the experience of sexual harassment and the eventual sexual assault of people in military units.

"When we did go into the focus groups, we asked a bit more about whether those rates seemed about right," Ms. Van Winkle explained. "And the feedback we got was that yes, they seemed about right."

What's more, "In fact, many said, 'We're surprised it's not higher,'" she said. "So this is where we started to see that culture that we've been discussing."

These sorts of sexist comments are particularly troubling to Pentagon officials because, "There is a strong positive correlation between the experience of sexual harassment and the eventual sexual assault of people in military units," said Nathan Galbreath, the Pentagon's senior executive adviser to SAPRO.

"And so we think that because these two problems are on the same continuum of harm, getting at that sexual harassment—the crude and sexist behavior—is part of the prevention work [for] sexual assault."

The focus-group comments of the cadets offer some insights into why the cadets themselves think the problem is pervasive, and how to best handle it.

When sexual harassment and assaults are prosecuted on campus, they think it might be a good idea to publicize them a bit more, even while protecting the anonymity of victims.

"When these things happen, my concern is, Are they being at all like hushed up?" one West Point cadet told Pentagon interviewers. "I think if we wanted to raise awareness and like say that this is a problem, why isn't it being publicized when it does happen, even anonymously?"

Predators in the Ranks

Pentagon researchers also wanted to know from cadets whether they thought unwanted sexual contact was a problem perpetrated by many fellow cadets, or by a few problem cadets. Military officials have gotten heat from lawmakers, for example, for being resistant to the idea of predators in the ranks.

Female cadets at West Point noted that in some cases, there are one or two well-known seniors in a company "that has made passes at most of the plebe girls. And they all have this uncomfortable feeling around him." That said, one female cadet added, "I don't think there are a lot of males here like that."

Female cadets also reported struggling with how to best handle put-downs and sexually harassing comments, while still being "cool."

"If someone touches you," one female cadet explained, there is an unspoken understanding that "you don't want to be like that girl and freak out about it." The question is how to let a fellow cadet know, "Hey, that's not cool, don't do it," she told Pentagon interviewers.

"You almost have to make that character judgment and decide in your mind if you think it's worth it."

Cadets of both genders feel that because the physical standards for female cadets are not as strenuous as those for male cadets, the men may have less respect for the women.

Because female cadets are far outnumbered by their male counterparts, one female cadet reported struggling with feelings of "maybe I am overreacting." She continued, "So I don't know what to do when everybody else seems to be okay with it."

While many women said they feel comfortable speaking up when they feel harassed, they also recognized that many female cadets also blame themselves when they experience unwanted sexual touching. "It starts to seem like the victim's fault for not being assertive," one said.

Different Standards

A clear theme that comes through in the survey, too, is that cadets of both genders feel that because the physical standards for female cadets are not as strenuous as those for male cadets, the men may have less respect for the women.

"The only thing I can think of is because some standards for women are lower," one male cadet told investigators. "My summer training, what I did last summer, girls aren't allowed to go to it because it's a male-only role."

"I think I saw it during 'Beast' a lot," said one female cadet, referring to the grueling summer training for freshmen. "If the female is slowing down the squad because they're having a harder time carrying the ruck, it sparks that negative mindset, like 'Why are the women in the military? Our entire unit is slowed down.' I can see frustration with that."

Another female cadet noted that because the physical standards are different for men and women at the academies, it is possible for women to get higher scores than men—even though they might not have to do as many push-ups or run a mile as quickly. "That eats him alive," said one female cadet of a male cadet friend of hers.

Until the Pentagon allows women to compete with men for the same combat jobs in the military, that culture of disrespect will continue, says Greg Jacob, a former US Marine and policy director for the Service Women's Action Network, in an interview. "Until women become full-fledged members of a team, and the more women get promoted up the chain of command—that's really the culture change that we're looking to see happen," he says.

Confronting the problem within the Pentagon, and at the service academies, remains "a daunting task," said Snow, who recently took over as director at SAPRO. "I've lost a lot of sleep in my first week on the job."

9

Men Are Often the Victims of Sexual Assault in the Military

Leonora LaPeter Anton

Leonora LaPeter Anton is a staff writer for the Tampa Bay Times.

Most discussions of military sexual assault focus on women, but in fact more men than women suffer assault in the military. Men can have an especially hard time coming forward to discuss sexual violence, and the trauma can haunt them for years. The military has not always done well with helping victims, who can be stigmatized and shamed for speaking out. The US Department of Veterans Affairs (VA) is working to do better in helping victims of sexual assault and has introduced some changes, including separating sexual assault survivors from veterans who suffer from combat posttraumatic stress disorder (PTSD).

Richard Bell Jr. was hanging up his polo shirts in his metal locker, when his new roommate walked in.

The two men regarded each other warily.

A nurse had told Bell, 65, that his roommate was gay. This was not something he wanted to hear. Bell, a grandfather of four, was "homophobic." In 1969, while in the Air Force in Thailand, a gang of men sexually assaulted him. He had come here to heal. How would this help?

Nelson Rivera, a short, thin Puerto Rican with his own palette of fears, cringed at the sight of the tall, quiet black man with sunken eyes. Bell resembled one of Rivera's drill sergeants from 35 years before, the first man who had raped him.

Rivera broke the awkward silence. The mess hall was around the corner, he explained, next to the library. The homeless vets were in one wing, those with substance abuse and combat-related psychological problems down another. Rivera and Bell were among 16 veterans housed in a wing of the Bay Pines VA Healthcare System devoted to military sexual trauma. They didn't know it, but their treatment had already begun.

That night, Bell went to bed early. He wrapped himself up in his blankets "like a Mexican taco," Rivera would later say.

Bell couldn't sleep that night in early May. He was supposed to stay eight weeks. He wasn't sure he wanted to stay the night.

[Bay Pines] is the only residential program in the country where men with military sexual trauma are housed and treated together and not mixed with veterans suffering other psychological problems.

Male Victims

In May, the Pentagon released the results of an anonymous survey on sexual assault in the military. An estimated 26,000 active duty service members reported they had been sexually assaulted or harassed in 2012, up from 19,000 in 2010. The numbers lent credence to descriptions of military sexual assault as a "crisis" and an "epidemic."

As far back as the 1991 Tailhook scandal, in which drunken aviators assaulted dozens of female recruits at a Las Vegas convention, attention on sexual assault in the armed forces has focused predominantly on female service members. Less widely publicized is that more than half of the victims in the recent survey—53 percent—were men.

This is not surprising to the mental health professionals at Bay Pines, where a decade ago a women-only program was expanded to include beds for men. It is the only residential program in the country where men with military sexual trauma are housed and treated together and not mixed with veterans suffering other psychological problems.

Carol O'Brien heads all programs dealing with post-traumatic stress disorder at Bay Pines. She has long recognized the need to treat male sexual trauma victims.

"It became clear to me," O'Brien said, "how very alone they felt in all of this."

Bell's journey to Bay Pines began in 2010, when, suffering from prostate cancer, he went to see a doctor at a VA outpatient clinic in Atlanta. The doctor asked him a question that has been routine at VA hospitals since 2000: had he been sexually assaulted while in the military?

It was the first time anyone had asked Bell this question and the answer caught in his throat. "No," he said.

As a younger man, he drank the thoughts away. His anger came out at bars. He'd get in his car and drive down the road at 100 mph, running red lights.

He blamed himself for everything that went wrong, then graduated to doubting himself, even when everything went right. He married and had three kids. He quit drinking. He buried himself in his job at Kennedy Space Center. He worked on the space shuttles until the *Challenger* blew up and then he moved to Georgia to work for Lockheed Martin.

When his mother died, he didn't grieve. When his beloved grandmother died, he didn't grieve. When he retired in 2003, his symptoms worsened and he withdrew further. He spent more and more days in bed.

The Department of Defense Annual Report on Sexual Assault in the Military suggests that less than 15 percent of service members who are sexually assaulted actually report it. Fewer men report than women.

Some male victims report being threatened with death or a duty change if they file a complaint. Some sexual assaults have been part of a hazing ritual and recruits may think they are violating a "code of silence." Others don't think anything will be done, so they don't bother.

That day in the doctor's office, Bell realized he'd said nothing for more than 40 years.

Not everyone who is raped gets PTSD. But those who do often let negative beliefs and thoughts take over their personalities.

"Yes," he corrected himself. He had been sexually assaulted. The doctor made a notation in his chart.

Assault and PTSD

A few weeks later, Bell took a seat in front of a therapist at the VA in Atlanta.

She explained that not everyone who is raped gets PTSD. But those who do often let negative beliefs and thoughts take over their personalities. They blame themselves for what happened and avoid the memory completely. Everywhere they look, they see danger. They are easily angered. They withdraw.

Bell nodded. That was him.

"What types of things do you find yourself avoiding," she asked.

"Anything that involves people, I don't want to be involved with," he said dejectedly. "I'm just one big hunk of . . . just negative, and I can't figure out why."

The therapist told Bell she'd help him "process the memory." She wanted him to undergo prolonged exposure, one of the primary treatments embraced by the U.S. military for post-traumatic stress disorder and rape.

She told Bell he would have to record the memory of his sexual attack in vivid detail and listen to the recording over and over at home to desensitize himself to it. He might tell his wife, his family. But all that was in the future. Now she asked him to close his eyes, tell her what happened.

Bell had spent so long avoiding this memory, he wasn't sure how much he could remember. He joined the Air Force in 1967 right out of high school, went overseas to Thailand, and worked his way up to sergeant in charge of a crew of Thai nationals who did construction work around the base.

It was hot, I was just getting back from lunch, he began.

He remembered he was wearing his fatigues, carrying his cap. There was a lot of laughter. He was crying. His memory faltered.

He opened his eyes. His therapist was watching him.

"Take it from the top," she said. Start over.

The prolonged exposure sessions with Bell's therapist in Atlanta were excruciating and ultimately not completely successful. In the quiet of his home in Kennesaw, Ga., he skipped his homework. His unhappy wife, still unaware of the true cause of his problems, asked him to schedule an appointment with a marriage counselor.

During a private one-on-one session, the counselor recommended Bell go to Bay Pines. It took about four months to make it off the waiting list.

Those first few days at Bay Pines, Bell kept to himself. The military sexual trauma program is set up more like a mini-college than a psych ward. Sixteen patients—roughly half men, half women—attend classes with names like coping skills, PTSD education and music therapy.

Bell met daily with his therapist, who asked him to write about his attack and how it made him feel. Bell found it easier than listening to the recordings of his anguished voice retell the most horrible day of his life.

Remembering the Assault

On a humid weekday in early June, Bell sat down with me in an air-conditioned office at Bay Pines, trying to put words to something he still hadn't told his wife of 31 years.

He swallowed and let his gaze settle on a white wall to the left.

At least a dozen men surrounded him. He realized it was the work crew. They held his arms. Then some of them grabbed his legs.

"One day after lunch, I came into the office and the Thai supervisor was there and he said, 'Sgt. Bell, I need to see you in the warehouse.'"

Bell described himself following the man into the dark, damp building. As he spoke, he looked beaten down. He knew he was not supposed to feel shame. And yet he did.

"I walk in and these hands grab me and startle me," he said. "I heard laughter. I thought someone was playing a joke."

At least a dozen men surrounded him. He realized it was the work crew. They held his arms. Then some of them grabbed his legs. They lifted him.

Bell's voice, normally so resonant, was so low I could barely hear him. He couldn't look at me. He seemed in physical pain.

"Are you okay?" I asked.

He nodded quickly. I realized he was forcing himself to tell me, that this was part of his therapy.

"Someone was undoing my belt buckle," he continued.

"I don't like this. I need to get loose." Bell was screaming now. "I want to fight. It's starting to get creepy and scary and I'm fighting. I'm twisting and turning. They have my feet in the air."

They pulled his pants down, then his underwear.

Bell paused. I held my breath.

Just then, O'Brien, the PTSD director, knocked on the door, interrupting us. She wanted to know how much longer the interview would take.

After she left the room, Bell resumed the story, skipping to the moment when he stood fully clothed in the warehouse, crying. "I was embarrassed, I was afraid and I was angry."

He stopped reporting for work, got drunk. He lost his three stripes and was jailed. Eventually, he got out of the military and returned to the United States.

"For me, my whole life has been like I was a zombie," Bell said. "I've spent it just trapped and going through the motions.

"I was alive and I was breathing," he said, "but I almost had to kill all my emotions . . . to keep myself from getting angry."

One day in late June, Bell and a couple of other veterans headed to a French bakery during a break between classes.

"Right now, I'm midway through my treatment and I feel like ripping my heart out," said Shilo Schluterman, a 37-year-old airplane mechanic from Arkansas in the Air National Guard. Schluterman, a pixieish woman, had been repeatedly sexually harassed, assaulted and groped while in the Air National Guard. She also suffered from combat-related PTSD from tours in Iraq and Afghanistan.

They put you in situations where normally you would be uncomfortable, but it turns out you learn a lot from it.

"I can say that all the fear that I went into my prolonged exposure with has diminished," said Jeffrey Palmer, 48, a father of four from Pennsylvania. He'd been raped by an armory sergeant in Germany in 1982, right when he got in the Army. "I'm not as scared to listen to my story anymore."

In addition to facing what had happened to them over and over, there were daily exercises to confront their fears. Bell joined several other vets for *Man of Steel* to conquer his fear of dark theaters. He went on a treasure hunt at the mall to overcome his fear of people and public places.

"They put you in situations where normally you would be uncomfortable, but it turns out you learn a lot from it," Schluterman said.

Bell agreed. His pairing with Rivera, the gay man who was afraid of black men, seemed like an attempt to make him and Rivera face their most feared archetypes. It had worked. They'd become friends.

Toward the end of his treatment, Bell was sitting in the screened porch behind the dormitory with a skinny guy from Connecticut named Jeff Wood.

Like Bell, Wood had been very young when he was assaulted. He was a 21-year-old Army medic stationed in Michigan. One day a lieutenant colonel suggested he go train in orthotics.

Weeks later, the lieutenant colonel picked Wood up by plane and flew him to Chicago to sign up for the training. Wood says once in Chicago, the man drove him to his house and kept him there for an entire weekend, raping him over and over. Wood said he froze. The man held all the power. Afterward, the commander signed his orders for the orthotics school.

After Wood graduated first in his class in orthotics and chose to be stationed in Hawaii, Wood said the lieutenant colonel called and asked him to dinner. Wood didn't show up and the next morning, he said, his orders were changed to Fort Benning, Ga.

Like Bell, Wood snuffed out the memory, told no one. He was discharged from the Army, built an orthotics business in Connecticut, married, became a drunk and ultimately lost everything.

"I always felt like one of those suburban houses with a white picket fence and a manicured lawn," Wood told Bell. "On the outside, everything looked smooth."

Bell nodded.

What might have happened if they'd addressed their trauma sooner, Wood wondered. Bell thought about it. He might have become a college graduate with an advanced degree. But what if he hadn't met his wife?

"I might not have had my kids," Bell said.

"I might not have lost my marriage," Wood said.

Finally Seeking Help

Listening to these decades-old stories of pain and dysfunction, I began to wonder why more victims, especially those who had been assaulted more recently, weren't seeking treatment.

All eight of the patients who talked to me, with the exception of Schluterman, had been raped between 20 and 40 years ago.

O'Brien, the PTSD chief, explained that it's hard to get people to come in, particularly men. It takes, on average, five years to seek help if they do get help at all. Most refuse to talk about their trauma with anyone.

In the military world, you have a system designed to almost destroy a victim who brings a complaint forward.

Also, many service members fear any sort of mental health evaluation, even for sexual assault, because many of those who have come forward have lost their security clearances, said Taryn Meeks, a former attorney with the Navy Judge Advocate General's Corps.

"We have some victims who have been labeled with 'a personality disorder,'" said Meeks, now executive director of Protect Our Defenders, a group dedicated to eliminating military sexual assault. "That's one of the reasons they are not seeking help now."

If they do implicate someone, the accused service member's commander decides if the case is prosecuted, Meeks said.

"In the military world, you have a system designed to almost destroy a victim who brings a complaint forward," said Paula Coughlin, the first female whistle-blower in the 1991 Tailhook scandal. She now operates a yoga studio in Jacksonville.

Coughlin, a former U.S. Navy lieutenant and helicopter pilot, described herself as "acute" and at times suicidal after the attack. The men formed a gauntlet through which dozens of women passed. The men tried to remove Coughlin's skirt and underwear and she was groped.

After speaking out, she came under attack by co-workers, superiors, even retired veterans she encountered in the grocery store. She heard every day that she had destroyed the Navy.

She said she went to a military counselor but learned the notes from her treatment were being passed to her commanders.

"Why would you seek mental health counseling," she asked, "from the same organization that destroyed you?"

In most programs, the sexual trauma patients are mixed in with veterans suffering combat distress, who sometimes look down on them.

Get Help Sooner

As he readied to depart Bay Pines, Bell said the treatment he got there had helped him heal. He'd never been able to remember what happened after the Thai workers grabbed him. His therapist suggested the gap in his memory might be his way of dealing with it.

Once he got home, Bell planned to return to bowling, start going to church again, perhaps jog, appreciate his wife more. He wished he'd come in sooner to reclaim himself.

He urged other sexually assaulted vets to get help sooner. Most service members who seek help from the Department of Defense or the Department of Veterans Affairs will receive outpatient treatment like the kind Bell received in Atlanta.

Nationwide, the VA has reserved 51 beds at six locations for military sexual trauma victims. The majority of those spots go to women.

In most programs, the sexual trauma patients are mixed in with veterans suffering combat distress, who sometimes look down on them. At Bay Pines, they are segregated into different wings but have a PTSD education class together.

"We both suffer PTSD, but when they put us together, our focus is on military sexual trauma," Bell said, "and the combat folks, some of them can be disrespectful and say things that set you back."

A few days before Bell was to leave, his father, stepmother, stepsister and daughter showed up in the Bay Pines parking lot to visit him. Bell was excited but nervous. None of them knew why he was here. He thought he'd tell them on the beach but first they stopped at John's Pass for pizza.

Once settled around the table, his stepsister asked him how he'd found Bay Pines and suddenly the whole story spilled out there on the sidewalk while dozens of families with kids in strollers streamed by.

"The reason I'm here is," Bell said, looking at his father, "I don't know if I mentioned it to you or not, Daddy, but it's military sexual trauma."

His family, unused to him talking so much, listened attentively.

"You know, I know now I didn't do anything wrong, but how do you tell somebody some men raped you?" Bell said.

As he spoke, the wind picked up and the sky turned gray. An American flag whipped in the stormy breeze. It started raining.

"I knew something wasn't right," said his stepmother. "I just didn't know what it was." His father furrowed his brow, but said nothing.

"It makes sense," said Retinna, Bell's 34-year-old daughter. She got up and walked away for a moment, her eyes wet.

"It's been rough trying to keep a secret, you know?" Bell said.

The rain stopped. The pizza was gone. They got up to leave. Bell and his daughter walked arm in arm back to the car.

10

Ending DADT Has Contributed to Sexual Assault in the Military

Bob Unruh

Bob Unruh is a reporter for WorldNetDaily. He was formerly a journalist at the Associated Press.

Sexual assault, especially of men, is rising dangerously in the military. This is linked to the repeal of DADT ("Don't Ask, Don't Tell") and the decision to allow gays to serve openly in the military. It is also the result of efforts to integrate women into the armed forces and the refusal to have separate basic training for men and women. Such moves are undermining the strength and culture of the military. The repeal of DADT was pushed through by deceptive reports about support for ending the policy among military personnel.

While the full picture remains far from clear, signs of the ill effects of the Democrat-initiated law allowing homosexuals to serve in the U.S. military without hiding their sexual preference are beginning to appear.

Sexual Assault Is Rising

The newest reports, for Fiscal Year 2011, have just come out, and Elaine Donnelly, president of the Center for Military Readiness [CMR], immediately noted that sexual misbehavior is on the rise.

She has completed an analysis of the the reports, including the overall military assessment of sexual assaults as well as the army's Gold Book report, and it cites 515 rapes, 414 aggravated sexual assaults and 349 forcible sodomies documented by just the Criminal Investigation Command in 2011.

"Pentagon officials regularly praise their own work and proclaim undeserved 'success,' even though evidence of sexual misconduct, both consensual and non-consensual, continues to accelerate, year after year," she said.

"It is time to reconsider and change flawed policies that are weakening the culture of the only military we have."

In December 2010, Congress repealed the "Don't Ask Don't Tell" policy established by President Clinton that allowed homosexuals to remain in the military on the condition they not make a public issue of their sexual lifestyle.

The new law, for first time in U.S. history, allows homosexual members to openly acknowledge their sexual choices.

Non-consensual sodomy attacks for fiscal 2011 totaled 7 percent of the nearly 2,500 attacks cited on one military report.

Among the details in the reports: While, since 2006, 5 percent of the violent sexual assaults have been against men, recent reports now put that figure at 12 to 14 percent.

The Army said it is "currently monitoring same-gender sex crime for a potential increase in forcible sodomy and other sex offenses related to the disassociation of homosexuality from the crime itself."

Non-consensual sodomy attacks for fiscal 2011 totaled 7 percent of the nearly 2,500 attacks cited on one military report.

In several cases "the victim ceased cooperating with the military justice proceeding and the subjects were given no judicial punishment for consensual sodomy."

Other case descriptions from the Department of Defense included:

- "Male victim alleged that male subjects groped him through clothing and attempted sodomy with a broom handle."

- "Male victim alleged that male subject performed oral sodomy on him in bar bathroom while he was passing in and out of consciousness from drinking."

- "Male victim alleged that the male subject, National Guard soldier, took out his penis, and straddled his thigh in the motor poll while in Iraq."

Military Is Failing

One of the reports said 9 percent of the victims claimed to be victims of "non-consensual sodomy."

The more than 700 pages of the compiled reports, however, did not mention homosexuality.

Donnelly told WND [WorldNetDaily] that the statistics show a more than 20 percent increase in reported sexual assaults on males.

And she said researchers specifically announced plans to track numbers to monitor the increase, since "this category of homosexual conduct no longer is illegal."

"It's way too soon," she said, to come to definitive conclusions. But she said the "numbers have gone way up."

She said the military's efforts to deal with the complications of women in the ranks, which have been around for years, as well as the new issues of open homosexuality, are failing.

"What they need to do is get rid of gender-integrated basic training," she said. "That conclusion was drawn that it did [increase] and still is increasing disciplinary issues."

"If you don't learn the basics of discipline [in basic training], it won't happen later," she said.

Donnelly's organization just released its policy analysis drawing information from the Army "Gold Book" report on wartime personnel stress, the most recent annual report of the Defense Department Sexual Assault Prevention & Response Office [SAPRO], and a 2010 report on ship captain firings from the Navy.

"Both the Army 'Gold Book' released in January and the Defense Department SAPRO report released last Friday hid the bad news in plain sight. Instead of reconsidering social policies known to increase disturbing disciplinary problems, the Pentagon is pressing ahead with costly, time-wasting programs that are not working," she warned.

She said teams of professional sexual assault response counselors, untold hours of mandatory training, preemptive punishments, bureaucracy, conferences, meetings and feel-good gimmicks have produced:

- A hike of 22 percent since 2007 in the sexual assaults in all branches

- A doubling since 2006 of the number of violent attacks and rapes in the Army, from 663 in 2006 to 1,313 last year

- A "chilling trend" of violent sex crimes rising at the rate of 14.6 percent annually, "and the rate is accelerating"

- A 28 percent increase in the offense rate and a 20 percent increase in offenders from 2006–2011 in sex crimes in the active-duty Army

- A jump in male sexual assault victims from 10 percent in 2010 to 14 percent in confidential reports for 2011

- The need to fire senior enlisted Navy officers at the rate of nearly two per month because of sexual misconduct.

Donnelly explained the problem has been developing for some time. She cited the 1997 recommendation from the Kassebaum-Baker Commission for the Army to end the gender-integrated basic training, because it was "resulting in less discipline, less unit cohesion, and more distraction from training."

But the advice was ignored, she said.

Despite tangible evidence of failure, the same officials expect free-rein to implement policies that would worsen the situation.

Endangering Military Strength

And Navy Secretary Ray Mabus, even while noting that the military branch experiences three sexual assaults every day, called for observance of a "Sexual Assault Awareness Month" that included "adult interactive plays."

"Despite tangible evidence of failure, the same officials expect free-rein to implement policies that would worsen the situation. On Feb. 9, 2012, Pentagon briefers announced their intent to promote 'diversity' by incrementally implementing controversial recommendations of the Military Diversity Leadership Commission," she said.

The report said, "More than 20 years ago, male and female naval aviators partied wildly at the 1991 post-Persian Gulf War Tailhook convention in Las Vegas. The highly publicized scandal ruined the careers of hundreds of officers."

Now, "we are starting to see a military resembling Jenga Blocks—a table-top tower constructed of smooth wooden planks," the report continued. "Players remove planks from the bottom of the tower and load them on the top, destabilizing the structure until it buckles and falls. In the same way, severe budget cuts combined with social burdens loaded on top could irreparably weaken the culture and strength of our military."

The report said the next White House administration, to minimize damage and reverse course, should "put the needs of the military above 'diversity metrics.'" And the military should reinforce core values and policies that are known to reinforce personal discipline, it said.

Basic training also needs to be separate for genders, women should be exempt from direct ground combat units, and military policies should be "based on reality, not 'social fiction.'"

[A US inspector general's report] said numbers were combined to present the image that members of the military approved of Obama's plan for open homosexuality.

CMR has reported previously on the manipulation of government data that contributed to the Obama campaign to remove the ban on open homosexuality. It cited an inspector general's report marked "For Official Use Only" that said numbers were combined to present the image that members of the military approved of Obama's plan for open homosexuality.

It was the military's original and now-suspect report that famously was quoted as affirming "70 percent" of the nation's military members believe the repeal of the long-standing "Don't Ask, Don't Tell" practice of allowing homosexuals to serve as long as they kept their sexual lifestyle choices to themselves would have either "a neutral or positive impact on unit cohesion, readiness, effectiveness and morale."

However, the IG [Inspector General] in documents uncovered by Donnelly revealed the actual figures for military members were: those who believed the change would impact units "very positively" (6.6 percent), "positively" (11.8 percent), "mixed" (32.1 percent), "negatively" (18.7 percent), "very negatively" (10.9 percent) and "no effect" (19.9 percent).

The only way the 70 percent figure can be reached is to combine "very positively," "positively," "mixed" and "no effect."

But this combination counts people with "neutral positions" as favoring the change, Donnelly argued.

The Military Does Not Support Repeal

Donnelly explained that taking the same figures and lumping them on the other side with "negatively" and "very negatively" would produce a total of almost 82 percent of the soldiers who believe the results of the change would be "negative or neutral."

The IG report uncovered by Donnelly said exactly that:

> We considered that the primary source's likely pro-repeal sentiment was further demonstrated by his/her inclusion of the key 70 percent figure in the information provided to the Washington Post. . . . Had [the source] desired to further an anti-repeal bias for the article, he/she could likewise have combined four results categories from that same survey question to conclude that "82 percent of respondents said the effect of repealing the 'Don't Ask, Don't Tell' policy would be negative, mixed or no effect."

The Department of Defense and the Department of the Navy have failed to produce a single document despite numerous FOIA requests over the last two years for information to uncover the truth surrounding the congressional repeal of "Don't Ask, Don't Tell."

The Thomas More Law Center announced a federal FOIA [Freedom of Information Act] lawsuit against the Navy, seeking to obtain records that are expected to show intentional deception by the Pentagon "to gain congressional support for repeal of the 1993 law regarding open homosexual conduct in the military, usually called 'Don't Ask, Don't Tell.'"

The lawsuit is based on the IG report obtained by Donnelly, "which suggested that a distorted Pentagon study of homosexuals in the military was produced and leaked solely to persuade Congress to lift the ban on open homosexuality."

Erin Mersino, the attorney handling the blockbuster case, said the organization already has tried to obtain information.

"The Department of Defense and the Department of the Navy have failed to produce a single document despite numerous FOIA requests over the last two years for information to uncover the truth surrounding the congressional repeal of Don't Ask, Don't Tell," she said.

In one side effect that rebounded on the White House, a Senate committee, in an attempt to ensure the law conforms to the new policy, voted to repeal the ban in the military on bestiality, an issue that White House press secretary Jay Carney didn't consider a serious question.

The Senate quickly backtracked when its vote was revealed.

WND previously reported on CMR's uncovering of the Inspector General's report.

Misleading Congress

That documents how the co-chairman of the commission working on the assessment of the impact on the military, Jeh Johnson, "read portions of 'an early draft' of the executive summary . . . to a former news anchor, a close personal friend visiting Mr. Johnson's home" three days before service members even were given the survey.

"Contrary to most news accounts, the 'Comprehensive Review Working Group' process was not a 'study,'" Donnelly told WND. "Its purpose was to circumvent and neutralize military opposition to repeal of the law."

She described the study "was a publicly funded pre-scripted production put on just for show."

"The . . . report, completed on April 8, 2011, reveals improper activities and deception that misled members of Congress in order 'to gain momentum in support of a legislative change during the "lame duck" session of Congress following the November 2, 2010, elections,'" she wrote.

Donnelly explained that days before the survey was distributed, Johnson "was seeking advice from a 'former news anchor' on how to write the report's executive summary more 'persuasively.'"

Further, "The DoD IG report concluded that someone who 'had a strongly emotional attachment to the issue' and 'likely a pro-repeal agenda' violated security rules and leaked selected, half-true information to the *Washington Post*," she explained.

Within days of the military's repeal of its ban on open homosexuality, two members of Congress pointed out that the Department of Defense had failed to fulfill its obligations to prepare for the change.

The letter was from House Armed Services Committee Chairman Howard "Buck" McKeon, R-Calif., and Rep. Joe Wilson, R-S.C., the chairman of the personnel subcommittee.

It was addressed to Defense Secretary Leon Panetta, whose media office declined to respond to a WND request for comment.

11

DADT Enforced Silence and Enabled Sexual Assault

Derek J. Burks

Derek J. Burks is a researcher at the US Department of Veterans Affairs, Mental Health Services.

Lesbian and gay service members are often targeted for abuse and harassment because of prejudice and discrimination. Stigma can make it difficult to report such incidents, since revealing that one is lesbian or gay can result in official sanctions and further harassment. The "Don't Ask, Don't Tell" (DADT) policy, which prevented lesbians and gays from serving openly in the military, probably exacerbated abuse in the military. Lesbian and gay service members could be blackmailed to keep silent about abuse. In addition, research into abuse and programs to deal with it were difficult or impossible.

Owing to the lack of published studies and data on LGB [lesbian, gay, and bisexual] individuals in the military, the prevalence, incident rates, and other factors associated with sexually based crimes are largely unknown. Still, the Servicemembers Legal Defense Network (SLDN, 2003) documented over 4,600 incidents of antigay harassment (e.g., verbal abuse, physical abuse, death threats) toward LGB servicemembers from 1994 to 2002. In 2004, several researchers (K. Balsam, B. Cochran, and T. Simpson, as cited in American Psychological Association Joint Divisional Task Force on

Derek J. Burks, "Lesbian, Gay, and Bisexual Victimization in the Military: An Unintended Consequence of 'Don't Ask, Don't Tell,'" *American Psychologist*, October 12, 2011. Copyright © 2011 by the American Psychological Association. Adapted with permission.

Sexual Orientation and Military Service, 2009) obtained data from 445 LGB and transgender military veterans (64.7% male, 27.2% female, 8.1% transgender) in an anonymous, Internet-based survey. Within the study, which was non-probability based, participants responded to various items that included experiences of victimization in the military. Demographics included gay or lesbian (88.7%), bisexual (7.2%), heterosexual (1.2%), or "other" (2.9%). Experiences of discrimination and victimization in the military as related to sexual orientation were reported by almost half of respondents, with 47.2% indicating at least one experience of verbal, physical, or sexual assault. Moreover, of those sampled, 8% reported experiencing sexual assault and 8% reported experiencing physical assault within the military. Female respondents also reported more experiences of sexual victimization than did male respondents.

Amid high prevalence rates of antigay violence in general, LGB individuals live in an inherently dangerous environment and may reasonably assume possibilities of being targeted and harassed.

Lesbian, Gay, and Bisexual Victimization

In 2000, the DoD [Department of Defense] sponsored a large-scale study to assess the harassment or LGB servicemembers (Office of the Inspector General, 2000) via witness accounts. Surveys were administered to 71,570 respondents (84% male, 16% female) in all branches of the active-duty military. Active duty is usually suggestive of an extended period of time in which an enlisted individual or officer member actively serves in the military, on or off base (Street et al., 2011). Findings indicated that within the previous 12 months, 37% had witnessed (and/or experienced) one or more of eight events related to harassment and violence based on perceptions or suspicions that the victim was gay. Among the most severe of events, physical assault was witnessed and reported by 5.3% of respondents.

In 2010, the Office of the Secretary of Defense sponsored an update to RAND's 1993 study on sexual orientation and U.S. military personnel policy. This served to supplement the DoD's (2010d) comprehensive review of DADT [Don't Ask, Don't Tell] (discussed later in this article). In order to examine how LGB servicemembers are currently affected by DADT[1] and to obtain their attitudes about a DADT repeal, RAND (2010) obtained the perspectives of LGB servicemembers using a peer-to-peer, Internet-based survey. Probability sampling was not possible, as the DoD does not maintain listings of active duty LGB servicemembers and because DADT constrains servicemembers from verbalizing their sexual orientation. Thus, maintaining confidentiality was critical in that LGB servicemembers are still at risk of military discharge and loss of a military career should their sexual orientation become known by participating in such research. Certificates of confidentiality were obtained from the National Institutes of Health to address this challenge and offer the strongest protection possible. Certificates such as these prevent forced disclosure of identifiable research information in civil, legislative, or other proceedings, whether at federal, state, or local levels (DoD, 2010c; Westat, 2010a).

Characteristics of the sample included a disproportionate number of men (80%) to women (20%), mostly midgrade enlisted personnel, and a disproportionate number of officers (64%) to enlisted servicemembers (36%). The majority of LGB respondents (91%) indicated that DADT puts gay servicemembers at risk for blackmail or manipulation, as well as negatively affects their personal (86%) and unit (76%) relationships. Seventy-two percent indicated experiencing stress

---

1. DADT was a policy which prevented gays and lesbians from serving openly in the military.

and anxiety in their daily lives because of DADT. Twenty-nine percent indicated having been teased or mocked and 7% indicated previous threats or injuries by other individuals in the military because of their own LGB sexual orientation. These perspectives are not statistically representative of all LGB servicemembers, but they nonetheless provide valuable information for the overall comprehensive review (RAND, 2010). . . .

Underreported Victimization

Amid high prevalence rates of antigay violence in general, LGB individuals live in an inherently dangerous environment and may reasonably assume possibilities of being targeted and harassed (Todahl, Linville, Bustin, Wheeler, & Gau, 2009). Among samples of LGB individuals, some who experienced sexual victimization also experienced negative consequences associated with reporting the incidents, such as being "outed," as well as negative reactions by the individual's social network (Todahl et al., 2009). Such experiences not only contribute to fears of reporting their victimization to law enforcement but may also contribute to the decision to not participate in research (Otis, 2007).

> *Encapsulated in a cycle of fear and potential extortion, LGB servicemembers may face threats ultimately leading to the experience of sexual victimization.*

Victims are likely to underreport their experiences of sexual assault and harassment (Turchik & Wilson, 2010). However, individual and group differences may also influence the decision to report or not report the incident. For example, victims who are female will likely face unique issues and considerations as compared to male victims, who will have their own unique issues to consider in deciding whether or not to report the victimization (Sivakumaran, 2005). In general, incidents of sexual assault and harassment in the military are reported by women at rates disproportionate to those for men (e.g., Street, Gradus, Stafford, & Kelly, 2007; Street, Stafford, Mahan, & Hendricks, 2008). Demographic information from a DoD (2010b) report on military sexual assault indicates that among 1,569 investigations during the 2009 fiscal year, the majority of victims were female (89%) and the majority of perpetrators were male (87%). The majority of victims as well as perpetrators were from junior enlisted ranks (E1 to E4) in comparison with higher ranking senior enlisted servicemembers (E5 to E9) and officers (O1 to O10). Analysis of perpetrator-on-victim gender among 1,512 of the investigations indicates that 79% were male on female, 6% were male on male, and less than 2% were female on male and/or female on female. Even though these rates suggest that gender is a unique risk factor for sexually based crimes, difficulties in reporting such crimes may also be moderated by gender. For example, male victims of sexually based crimes, in general, report such crimes less often than do their female counterparts (Sivakumaran, 2005, 2007). Moreover, victims who are gay or lesbian may believe they have even fewer options for help. Some may believe they could be further harmed if the action of seeking help were to draw attention to their LGB sexual orientation (an inadvertent double disclosure) and/or served to increase the likelihood of subsequent revictimization.

Issues surrounding sexual stigma, sexual victimization, and DADT likely intertwine to increasingly prevent LGB servicemembers from feeling safe enough to report victimization and/or seek assistance and support, because there is no guarantee of confidentiality from other military personnel (Frank, 2004; Johnson & Buhrke, 2006). According to Hunter (2007),

Other than threats of death, the fear of being labeled homosexual is the most powerful psychological dynamic that prevents men who have been sexually abused from reporting it to military authorities. Since male victims of sexual assault, whether heterosexual or homosexual, are even less likely to report it than female victims, perpetrators can be confident they can get by with little fear of punishment or even even investigation.

Encapsulated in a cycle of fear and potential extortion, LGB servicemembers may face threats ultimately leading to the experience of sexual victimization (e.g., "Sleep with me or I will report that you are gay"). Subsequent threats by the perpetrators may serve to further contain the crime and prevent it from being reported (e.g., "If you tell anyone about this, I will 'out' you or hurt you even worse"). Thus, from the victim's perspective, not reporting may seemingly be the best way to avoid increased harm, distress, and other negative consequences, such as military discharge. . . .

Is "Don't Ask, Don't Tell" to Blame?

LGB individuals are a vulnerable population who experience disproportionately high reports of hate-related crimes and other victimization across the life span. Add to the formula an active-duty military environment, in which LGB individuals typically serve covertly, and harassment and violence become great sources of concern (Herek, 1993). DADT policy serves to negatively magnify an environment already characterized by conservative gender norms, heterosexism, and sexual stigma. It is known that LGB victimizations occur in the military whether or not LGB individuals are open. However, the extent of victimization is unknown. Further, whether or not the unique LGB characteristics of openness and outness serve to increase the risk for victimization is also unknown. LGB individuals are first and foremost at higher risk of victimization in the military because of their sexual orientation. Regardless of DADT, the same risk is probable; however, such policy moderates the risk by further promoting a climate of sexual secrecy that becomes even more discriminatory toward LGB servicemembers.

In addition, among servicemembers who are sexually victimized, DADT's influence likely exacerbates incidents of sexual trauma. In particular, victimized LGB servicemembers may fear even worse consequences in making a report or seeking health care services, which will also add to underreported rates of sexual victimization. Thus, we can deduce that, to an extent, DADT serves to increase disparities in LGB research and efforts to prevent sexual victimization. This is evident in the lack of attention given to sexual orientation as a risk factor in the extant military-based research on sexual assault and harassment. Because of DADT, military research linking sexual orientation with these forms of trauma cannot be conducted easily, if at all. And without scientific evidence, the extent of victimization cannot adequately be monitored, treatment efforts cannot be fully implemented, and policy initiatives cannot adequately address sexually based crimes (Purdam et al., 2008). Given that LGB individuals face high rates of victimization in the general population and assumedly at least fair-to-moderate rates in the military (based on limited, non-peer-reviewed research), increased research seems more than justified. What's more, researchers and health care providers are encouraged to examine and work through their own fears and stigma related to approaching LGB issues. Although that is perhaps more easily suggested than done, it is likely that the level of fear and worry they feel is relatively less than the level felt by LGB servicemembers, especially those who have been victimized.

12

Sexual Harassment and Assault More Likely for Women Who Saw Combat

Wyatt Olson

Wyatt Olson is a reporter for Stars and Stripes.

A Pentagon study shows that women in the military who had combat-like experiences were also more likely to have encountered sexual harassment or sexual abuse. Researchers believe that troops in combat situations, in which they are under greater stress, have less accountability. Also because there are fewer women in combat units, they are likely to be the targets of sexual harassment and abuse. The services hope that the report will help them better target and confront sexual harassment.

Deployed women who underwent "combat-like" experiences in Iraq and Afghanistan are much more likely to report sexual harassment and sexual assault compared with other deployed women, according to a new study.

Deployment and Harassment

Published in the August edition of *Women's Health Issues* journal, the study used data from more than 13,000 military women who have been tracked in the Millennium Cohort Study, which began in 2001. Participants filled out an extensive "baseline" questionnaire and repeat the Defense Department research survey at three-year intervals.

Sexual assault of women in the military has become a major focus for the Pentagon and the service branches. Victims have called on the Defense Department and Congress to take effective steps to curb assaults and prosecute perpetrators.

Women account for about 200,000 of the military's 1.4 million active-duty personnel, according to Pentagon figures. More than 280,000 women have deployed in Afghanistan and Iraq since the 9/11 attacks, and women will likely see more combat after the Defense Department rescinded a rule barring them from combat positions earlier this year. The DOD plans to integrate them into those jobs by 2016.

The youngest deployed women, born after 1980, were more than five times more likely to report sexual assault than their older counterparts.

The journal study is the first to use such a broad-based group of female servicemember—including reserve and National Guard personnel—to analyze the association between "sexual stressors" and deployments in Iraq and Afghanistan.

Cynthia LeardMann, a researcher with the Naval Health Research Center in San Diego who co-authored the journal article, said the study increases data "about where we can specifically help provide interventions and prevention programs" so the military can "target certain environments, as well as, perhaps, certain service branches."

The study categorized stressors as sexual harassment, sexual assault or a combination.

Women were considered to have combat-like experience if they witnessed at least one of these: death, physical abuse, dead or decomposing bodies, maimed soldiers or civilians, or prisoners of war or refugees.

Deployed women exposed to combat-like experiences reported a 20 percent incidence rate of sexual harassment and a 4 percent rate of sexual assault during the three-year follow-up period after the baseline questionnaire.

While the study could not pinpoint the reported sexual stressor as happening during deployment, LeardMann said that the researchers were "pretty confident" that incidents such as witnessing death or rotting corpses would likely be during deployment.

The study also found that the youngest deployed women, born after 1980, were more than five times more likely to report sexual assault than their older counterparts.

Targeting Prevention

Rates of sexual harassment and assault varied by branch of service. For example, the rate of sexual harassment for women in the Air Force and Navy was the lowest at 5.8 percent. That rate in the Army was 10.3 percent, with the Marines having the highest at 13.3 percent.

Female Marines also reported the highest rate of sexual assault at 6.6 percent, compared to 1.6 percent reported by Air Force women.

The authors offered possible explanations for increased sexual harassment/assault during deployment.

"Women who experience combat while deployed are not only in more stressful and dangerous circumstances but they may also find themselves in more traditionally male-dominated environments compared with other deployed women," the study said.

"Furthermore, in these high-stress and often life-threatening environments, prioritizing the identification and prevention of sexual stressors may be more challenging, perpetrators may be less concerned with consequences of committing assault, and perpetrators may be less likely to be held accountable for their actions."

The study did not collect information on the perpetrators of reported sexual harassment/assault.

The researchers discovered that women who had been deployed before the baseline questionnaire reported far fewer experiences of sexual harassment and assault.

"Some of this we believe to be a selection effect," Leard-Mann said. "That is, women who have experienced sexual trauma are probably more likely to leave service. So it could be that those women who have had a prior experience are more likely to get out; therefore, the women who are left in our population to continue to serve in the military are going to be less likely to experience another event or haven't experienced it in the past because they are the ones who stayed in."

Because the findings indicate that risk factors are related to the type of environment—such as combat experience and branch of service—and to "resiliency factors" such as changes in marital status, the study concludes it would be wise to target prevention efforts in these areas.

13

Ending the Ban on Women in Combat May Reduce Sexual Assault

Carey L. Biron

Carey L. Biron is a Washington, DC correspondent with IPS and Mint Press News, reporting on development, accountability, and international governance.

The US military is moving to rescind the ban on women in combat. It is hoped that treating women equally in the armed forces will reduce sexual assaults and harassment. Currently, the ban on women in combat and from some careers in the military sends the message that women are second class and unequal. This in turn creates a culture of misogyny in which harassment is often tolerated. Experts and military commanders say that creating a more equal military should lead to more equal treatment for all.

Following on a surprise announcement, U.S. Secretary of Defence Leon Panetta on Thursday confirmed that the U.S. military will be rolling back a nearly two-decade-old ban on women in the U.S. military serving in frontline combat positions.

Ending the Ban

"Women have shown great courage and sacrifice on and off the battlefield," Panetta said. "The (Defence) Department's goal in rescinding the rule is to ensure that the mission is met with the best-qualified and most capable people, regardless of gender."

Since the 1994 ban went into effect, but particularly since the start of the war in 2001 in Afghanistan, critics have warned that the policy has made it more difficult for women to move up in the military ranks. Simultaneously, it misses out on the fact that female troops are already serving and dying in hazardous posts throughout U.S. combat operations.

Some have also suggested that the ban is partially to blame for a spate of sexual assaults that have plagued the military. Last year, Panetta suggested that the number of sex assaults in the U.S. armed forces could be as high as 19,000 a year.

"The military has long been a culture of misogyny. As long as military women did not have equal treatment from the top—the Pentagon—they were often treated as second class at best, sexual prey at worst," Helen Benedict, author of "The Lonely Soldier: The Private War of Women Serving in Iraq" and a journalism professor at Columbia University, told IPS.

"Disrespect lies at the root of misogyny, and misogyny lies at the root of sexual assault. A culture takes a long time to change, but officially recognising women as equal will help to change it."

The more we can treat people equally, the more likely they are to treat each other equally.

Speaking with Panetta at the public announcement on Thursday, General Martin Dempsey, the head of the Joint Chiefs of Staff, which spearheaded the new policy change, acknowledged that the U.S. military has an "ongoing issue with sexual harassment and sexual assault."

"I believe that's because we've had separate classes of military personnel," Dempsey said. "When you have one part of the population that's designated as warriors and another part that's designated as something else, I think that disparity begins to establish a psychology that in some cases led to that environment."

He continued: "I have to believe the more we can treat people equally, the more likely they are to treat each other equally."

Reflecting Service

Thursday's announcement has been widely lauded, with many calling the move long overdue.

Although the U.S. military continues to be made up predominantly of men, over the past two decades the number of women in the armed forces has risen steadily. Today, women constitute around 15 percent of all personnel in active service, some 1.4 million people.

Over the past decade-plus of war in Iraq and Afghanistan, more than 280,000 women have been deployed. And, according to the Defence Department, since 2001 at least 140 U.S. women soldiers have been killed and 865 have been wounded in those conflicts, in what analysts have repeatedly referred to as wars without frontlines.

"This is a tremendous victory for equality and justice in our military," Anu Bhagwati, executive director of the Service Women's Action Network (SWAN) and a former Marine Corps captain, said in a statement. "Women's service in Iraq and Afghanistan set the stage for this—the policy on the books simply did not reflect the reality of women's service."

Bhagwati also noted the importance of a recent lawsuit brought by SWAN and the American Civil Liberties Union (ACLU) in putting pressure on the Pentagon.

According to the lawsuit, the ban on women in combat positions "categorically excludes (women) from more than

200,000 positions, as well as from entire career fields. Consequently, commanders are stymied in their ability to mobilize their troops effectively."

The ACLU also warned that servicewomen were being "denied training and recognition for their service, put at a disadvantage for promotions, and prevented from competing for positions for which they have demonstrated their suitability and from advancing in rank."

The United States lags behind many other Western countries in terms of allowing women in combat rolls. A British government report from 2009 called out only the U.S., U.K. and Australia as continuing to maintain exclusion policies on women.

Ameliorating Disrespect

Importantly, Thursday's announcement comes following a broad review at the highest levels of the military, indicating that the top brass is in general support of the changes. (Secretary Panetta is a civilian appointed by President Obama, who on Thursday stated his "strong support" for the policy change.)

Thursday's decision comes after the military weakened the ban slightly last year, opening up 14,000 additional positions to women. It also follows the recent repeal of the controversial Don't Ask, Don't Tell legislation that had disallowed gay and lesbian soldiers from disclosing their sexuality. "Just as the lifting of Don't Ask, Don't Tell removed official permission to bully and persecute gays and lesbians," Helen Benedict told IPS, "so will the lifting of the ban on women in ground combat help to ameliorate the disrespect with which they have so long been regarded." Still, the move has received some criticism, both from some Republican members of the U.S. Congress and from certain analysts worried about issues of privacy and how well men and women can work together in frontline situations.

On Monday, a group called the Center for Military Readiness released a lengthy report warning that the "Liberal media and feminists are trying to use the military as a laboratory for the testing of a controversial twentieth-century social science theory—that men and women are interchangeable in all roles, and any differences that do exist are primarily, if not exclusively, due to socialization."

Although Thursday's announcement indicates clear intention, it does allow for a significant period for potential tweaking. Panetta is requiring military heads to get back to him with implementation plans by May [2013], and they will have until 2016 to make final recommendations.

14

Sexual Assault Cases Should Be Removed from the Chain of Command

Lindsay Rosenthal and Lawrence Korb

Lindsay Rosenthal was formerly a research assistant with the health policy team and women's health and rights team at the Center for American Progress. She is now a fellow with the Ms. Foundation for Women's advocacy and policy department. Lawrence Korb is a senior fellow at the Center for American Progress and an adjunct professor at Georgetown University.

Currently, sexual assault cases in the military are handled by the chain of command, and commanding officers can decide not to prosecute or modify verdicts. This is unjust. Commanding officers are not legally trained; in addition, they have an interest in not reporting, since they may face consequences if there are high rates of sexual assault in units under their command. It also places a burden on victims and violates their right to privacy if they have to report sexual assault to their superiors. Prosecution and handling of sexual assault cases should be placed either under civilian authority or under a separate military justice system, as is the case in many other countries throughout the world.

Removing dispositional authority from the chain of command is a critical step to address the military's sexual assault problem and has been at the center of the controversy over how best to address sexual assault in the military.

Lindsay Rosenthal and Lawrence Korb, *Twice Betrayed: Bringing Justice to the U.S. Military Sexual Assault Problem,* Center for American Progress, November 2013, pp. 28–34.

The Power of Commanders

The military criminal justice system is unique in that it currently allows commanders absolute discretion in decisions that determine whether an offender will be prosecuted for sexual misconduct and the ultimate consequence upon conviction. The Manual for Courts-Martial currently maintains that the officer who determines whether or not a criminal case goes to trial is in the chain of command of the service member accused of assault. Moreover, commanders—who lack legal training and have a conflict of interest—have the authority to overturn, lessen, or modify convictions. In just one example, earlier this year, an Air Force general officer overturned a fighter pilot's sexual assault conviction—which was decided by a panel of six colonels—on the basis that the attacker "adored his wife and 9-year old son." The incident became the center of a national controversy and demonstrated the longstanding flaws in allowing such command discretion in military criminal proceedings and led to the Senate Armed Services Committee voting to remove this authority.

Commanding officers and high-ranking military officials are often the perpetrators of sexual offenses in the military.

The ability of commanders to maintain order and discipline is critical to the readiness of the armed forces and U.S. military operations' success. Commanders need to know that their troops can carry out directed orders in the most stressful of conditions. But there is a difference between enforcing discipline and addressing criminality. Trained legal and law enforcement professionals should always address criminal behavior; that is the only way to ensure that the victim and defendant's rights to justice and due process are protected. Even if jurisdiction over criminal offenses were removed from commanders, they would still retain authority over minor crimes and authority to enact administrative punishments in order to enforce discipline within their units.

Commanders May Be Harassers

There are four facts that support removing dispositional authority for sexual assault cases from the chain of command.

First, commanding officers and high-ranking military officials are often the perpetrators of sexual offenses in the military. In 2012, the results of the WGRA [Workplace and Gender Relations Survey of Active Duty Members] found that 25 percent of service members who reported unwanted sexual contact said someone in their chain of command assaulted them. Another 38 percent reported that the offender was of a higher rank or pay grade but not in their chain of command. Altogether, this means 63 percent of service members who reported unwanted sexual contact on this year's WGRA survey were attacked by someone who outranks them.

This statistic has remained consistent over the several years that the WGRA has been administered. According to the *International Handbook of Violence Research*, as far back as 1988, the Pentagon conducted a survey of 20,000 male and female . . . troops on the subject of sexual harassment. Among female soldiers, 70 percent reported harassment, and among male soldiers, the figure was 36 percent. Surveyed women were twice as likely as men to be harassed by their direct military supervisors, at 21.9 percent versus 11.8 percent of men, or by other high-ranking military personnel, at 18.7 percent versus 8.6 percent.

Second, even when they are not the perpetrators, commanding officers have an inherent conflict of interest when it comes to prosecuting sexual assault cases. Since military commanders are evaluated on their command climate and are rated poorly if sexual assault takes place within their unit, it is not in a commander's best interest to even investigate allegations. No matter how high up in the chain of command one places dispositional authority, this conflict of interest still exists.

Third, even when victims do not fear direct retaliation from their commander, commanders must be given all information about the case in order to decide whether or not to go to court martial—including graphic information and details that may negatively impact the victims' career. This discourages victims from reporting the crimes committed against them. Victims want to move on with their military career and maintain as much normalcy in their job duties as possible. Having commanders determine whether or not to prosecute the case means that victims are forced to choose between maintaining their right to privacy from their commander or having the option to pursue justice through the military legal system.

Fourth, an officer's rank does not connote any expertise in legal matters. Trained legal professionals should be handling all criminal cases, particularly sexual assault cases that are exceptionally difficult to prosecute.

Reporting a crime as a soldier or sailor is more like reporting to an employer than to police.

In a letter to the chairman of the Senate Armed Services Committee, Adm. James Winnefeld defends keeping sexual assault cases within the chain of command by arguing that commanders prosecute cases more frequently than civilian prosecutors. The letter presents a tally of cases that the military prosecuted—often to a successful conviction—after civilian prosecutors "declined to prosecute." Prosecuting sexual assault and bringing justice to victims is not a race to the bottom; the military should not point to the failure of the civilian justice system to defend its own serious and systemic problems in its response to sexual assault.

In any case, because DOD [Department of Defense] has not made the supporting documents public, it is difficult to ascertain what the data presented in Adm. Winnefeld's letter actually mean. It is not clear whether the cases Winnefeld references were cases that civilian prosecutors would never have prosecuted. It is also not clear if they were cases involving overlapping jurisdiction between military and civilian prosecutors where authorities mutually agreed that the case should be retained in the military legal system.

Moreover, the question of whether civilian prosecutors decline cases at higher rates than commanders is irrelevant to the chain-of-command issue. No one is proposing placing the authority to prosecute crimes in the hands of civilian prosecutors or removing sexual assault cases from the jurisdiction of the UCMJ [Uniform Code of Military Justice]. Rather, the debate is over whether the military personnel responsible for prosecuting cases should be within the chain of command or whether the prosecutor should be a legally trained military professional operating in an independent office outside the chain of command. Adm. Winnefeld presented no evidence to suggest that commanders would be more likely to prosecute cases than other military lawyers who are not in the chain of command.

As Roger Canaff, a leading expert in prosecuting sexual violence who has provided training to the armed forces on how to prosecute sexual assault, made these points:

> [Some have] asserted "off-post rapes" committed by service members (and thus pursuable by both civilian and military prosecutors), are pursued by military prosecutors at far higher rates. This is a good thing, but not surprising. Off-post sex crimes committed by service people are usually committed against other service people and involve military witnesses. The military is in a better position to pursue those cases and has more interest in doing so. Civilian prosecutors' offices are also notorious for declining to pros-

ecute challenging sexual violence cases (i.e, the vast majority), so no one should be offering them (collectively) as a standard to be emulated. But again, how does a lackluster civilian response translate into the military having no serious issues with its response? Yes, the military prosecutes rape, and increasingly does so aggressively and competently.... But first a report must be made. This is a major response issue the military faces.... Reporting a crime as a soldier or sailor is more like reporting to an employer than to police. Sex crimes are difficult for anyone to report. Imagine reporting to a superior you work with everyday (while your attacker is in or near the very same environment) and then to a command stream where cohesiveness and unflagging enthusiasm are the most demanded attributes.... The efforts of Sen. Kirsten Gillibrand (D-NY) and Rep. Jackie Speier (D-CA), aim at addressing these realities with military lawyers, just outside the chain of command where inherent conflicts exist.

Why Increasing Checks on Command Authority Will Not Go Far Enough

The 2013 NDAA [National Defense Authorization Act] responded to the crisis of military sexual assault by elevating the initial dispositional authority for disciplinary actions on sexual assault cases to the rank of colonel or higher in the chain of command of the accused service member. The goal of the reform is to place accountability for prosecution with higher ranking officers who would theoretically make better decisions than lower ranking commanders about whether or not to proceed to court martial. The proposed 2014 NDAA would go a step further to address accountability by keeping dispositional authority at the elevated command level and adding an additional check on command authority. A proposal from Sen. Carl Levin (D-MI), chairman of the Senate Armed Services Committee, would preserve the 2013 requirement that sexual assaults are referred to an officer of the rank of colonel or higher within the accused service member's chain of command. But in the event of a JAG [Judge Advocate General] officer investigating a crime recommended that an alleged perpetrator be tried through general court martial and the commanding officer disagrees with that decision, the case would automatically be referred to the service secretary of the relevant branch for review of command's decision. The intent of the proposal is to create a substantial deterrent for commanders to go against the advice of the trained JAG in terms of how to proceed with the case while at the same time preserving final authority over the decision within the chain of command.

It is unlikely that a service secretary's review would really effect increasing accountability. The secretary, who may or may not be a lawyer or have any expertise in criminal law, would receive the file prepared by the JAG and commanding officer and likely would not reopen a case, interview witnesses, or otherwise engage in any independent investigation of the alleged offense. It is clear that top military leadership are inclined to support command authority, as evidenced by the Pentagon's adamant defense of maintaining authority within the chain of command. JAGs are aware of this preference on the part of the commanding officer and military leadership and ultimately may not have any real professional independence from the chain of command. The staff judge advocates with whom the commander would confer about whether or not to proceed to court-martial often work for and are evaluated by the commanding officer who is the convening authority rather than through an independent process in the JAG core. Therefore, as the proposal and the performance evaluation process are currently structured, the military prosecutor has a strong disincentive to trigger the automatic review on sexual assault cases, even if we were to assume that the service secretary is an objective and qualified reviewer in making this determination.

The 2014 NDAA will likely make a number of important changes, including addressing the abuse of Article 60 by stripping commanders of their ability to modify findings. It will likely take an important step to protect victims by making it a specific crime under the UCMJ to retaliate against victims. It also includes a number of administrative changes aimed at improving the SAPRO's [Sexual Assault Prevention and Response Office] response to sexual assault, such as asking the armed services to develop specific personnel criteria for SAPRO. But on the key issue of impacting accountability for perpetrators, the proposal included in the 2014 NDAA falls short by failing to entrust professional prosecutors with the crucial decisions about whether or not to prosecute sex offenses rather than officers—regardless of how high ranking they may be—who generally lack any legal training whatsoever and inevitably have a conflict of interest in the matter.

> *When it comes to sexual assault, the military's track record is getting steadily worse.*

International Precedent for Military Justice Outside of the Chain of Command

There is an established international precedent for taking the authority to prosecute sexual offenses out of the chain of command. Two different models have been implemented in the international community: taking authority out of the military justice system altogether and granting authority to civilian law enforcement and creating an independent criminal justice system within the military itself.

France and Germany are two examples of countries that have placed authority in civilian systems. Canada, the United Kingdom, and Israel have taken prosecutorial authority outside of the chain of command by creating independent judiciaries within their existing military structures. No evidence has been presented that the readiness or unit cohesion of these militaries has declined because commanders are not handling criminal cases. Under our status of forces agreement with Japan and South Korea, these countries can and do prosecute U.S. service personnel who commit crimes off base.

The Military Must Do Better

The military expects its members to exhibit conduct that demonstrates discipline and integrity. Such standards are based on high principles of character that reach well beyond the goal of weeding out criminal behavior. Every day, service members can and do conduct themselves in this way; but when it comes to sexual assault, the military's track record is getting steadily worse.

The public should not accept sexual assault in the military simply because assault is also prevalent in other institutions such as college campuses, as some have insinuated. The military is an exceptional institution in everyway—both because it has the tools to hold offenders in the military accountable and because service members must be held to the highest standards of conduct given the important responsibilities and privileges we entrust them with.

With military sexual assault numbers on the rise, it is imperative that military leaders and members of Congress leave no option off the table to end this shameful trend. Important changes have been made in recent years, and pending legislation takes important steps toward reform, including improving the experiences of survivors who report the crimes committed against them, improving training for military personnel, and increasing our understanding of the issues through important research. But holding offenders accountable is the key to the kind of drastic change that is necessary. The military has had more than two decades to prove that it can do so within the command structure; but it has failed to do so, at the expense of victims' safety and the integrity of our armed forces. The time has come to remove dispositional authority from within the chain of command and institute a credible and objective justice system.

15

Sexual Assault Cases Should Be Handled by the Chain of Command

Charles "Cully" Stimson

Charles "Cully" Stimson is the manager of the National Security Law Program at The Heritage Foundation's Davis Institute for International Studies.

The military's mission of defending the country is paramount and must be kept in mind when approaching the problem of sexual assault in the military. The chain of command is vital in combat and in accomplishing the military's mission. The chain of command provides the authority to deal aggressively with military sexual assault and will allow the military to prosecute and confront cases that would not be followed up by civilian authorities. The military can and must do better in eliminating sexual assault, but the best way to achieve that goal is through the current chain of command, not through a radical change in military justice.

The military exists to defend the nation. That is its mission. To accomplish that mission, leaders must ensure that those who serve under them are combat ready, and once ordered into armed conflict, combat effective. Maintaining good order and discipline in the armed forces is essential to accomplishing the mission.

Military Justice Is Different

The United States military justice system is integral to the military's mission. It is unique, and for good reason. Unlike the civilian justice system, which exists solely to enforce the laws of the jurisdiction and punish wrongdoers, our military justice system exists in order to help the military to succeed in its mission: to defend the nation. It is structured so that those in charge, commanding officers, can carry out the orders of their civilian leaders. Ultimately, it is structured to fight and win wars.

> *When proposing improvements to the military justice system, Congress must realize that the military is fundamentally different from the civilian world.*

Incidents of sexual assault are a real and recognized problem, both in the military and in civilian life. While studies suggest that the number of sexual assaults in the military may be less than the number in civilian society, sexual assault has a uniquely greater damaging effect on the military, such that even one incident is unacceptable. Incidents of sexual assault are detrimental to morale, destroy unit cohesion, show disrespect for the chain of command, and damage the military as a whole, both internally as well as externally. Service members are trained for situations in which it is essential to trust both enlisted members of the unit and the chain of command completely. Sexual assault in the military destroys that trust, which can detract from the readiness of America's armed forces.

However, before Congress enacts additional legislation to address the issue of sexual assault in the military, it should take stock of the facts. Over the past few years, the military services have made huge strides with regard to addressing the issue of sexual assault, including mandatory general military training for all personnel, specific training for select individuals, and many more specific programs aimed at the uniformed military lawyers responsible for prosecuting and defending sexual assault charges. The facts also demonstrate that the military has done an admirable job training and mentoring military prosecutors and defense counsel—training that is on par with the best practices in large city district attorney and public defender offices.

The military justice system is a well-developed, unique, and integrated criminal justice system, which handles thousands of criminal cases per year, ranging from minor violations to major felonies. In almost all of these cases the system works to ensure justice is done. It is not perfect, but neither is the civilian criminal justice system, which has many flaws and must be continually improved. However, when proposing improvements to the military justice system, Congress must realize that the military is fundamentally different from the civilian world.

Commanding officers in the military have a wide range of tools available to enforce good order and discipline. These include mild administrative remedies, such as informal counseling, formal counseling, Executive Officer Inquiry, and nonjudicial punishment under Article 15 of the Uniform Code of Military Justice. The ultimate remedy for any commanding officer is the power to immediately refer a suspected criminal in the chain of command to a court-martial.

Taking that power away from commanding officers eliminates an indispensable authority that cannot be delegated or transferred to another if we are to demand accountability from commanders for prosecuting and preventing sexual assaults and other serious crimes. This notion of accountability to one's commanding officer may seem mysterious to civilians who have never served in the armed forces. But chain of command, and accountability up and down the chain of command, is essential to carrying out the missions as ordered by the President, whose authority as Commander in Chief owes accountability to the people via elections and assures a military that will not threaten a constitutional democracy—whether our country is engaged in an armed conflict or not.

What removing the power to convene courts-martial from the commander would do is undermine all commanders' ability to enforce good order and discipline across the armed forces.

Undermining Good Order

Under the current system, commanders have the legal responsibility and authority to refer criminal suspects to a court-martial. They do so sometimes against the advice or recommendation of a military lawyer. The reason this sometimes happens is because commanders can refer cases to court-martial when they are convinced that there is probable cause that a crime has been committed and that the accused committed the crime. Prosecutors view cases through a different legal lens: they must be able to prove the case beyond a reasonable doubt.

Some proponents of the removal of command authority have identified as "success" stories similar policies in Canada, New Zealand, Australia, and the United Kingdom and urge the United States to follow suit. But these countries' removal of prosecutions from the chain of command can hardly be touted as a success for victims. In fact, most of our allies reported that removing the authority to prosecute from the chain of command has slowed prosecutions, and they saw no increase in the number of convictions under the new system.

What removing the power to convene courts-martial from the commander would do is undermine all commanders' ability to enforce good order and discipline across the armed forces. For example, combat commanders, when lawfully engaged in armed conflict, have the authority to order their soldiers to kill the enemy. The proposal would, among other things, eliminate those commanders' authority to prosecute those soldiers that indiscriminately kill women and children or commit other violations of the Law of Armed Conflict. In the words of a retired service member, "don't take the authority away from command; let's look at the processes that can support the commanders." As Senator Claire McCaskill (D-MO) said, "the best way to protect victims and realize more aggressive and successful prosecutions is by keeping the . . . chain of command in the process at the beginning of a criminal proceeding . . . there's no substitute for a commander who does it right." The Senator is correct.

In the past 50 years, Congress has formalized military justice rules and procedures through statute in a thoughtful and methodical manner, with a keen appreciation for the fact that the military justice system is uniquely calibrated to support the mission of the military.

In recent months, there have been congressional hearings, legislative proposals, debates, and an ongoing dialogue about how to address the issue of sexual assault in the military. The House has passed key reforms to the existing system in its version of the National Defense Authorization Act (NDAA), and the Senate will take up a variety of reform amendments this fall when it votes on the Senate NDAA. Some of the House and Senate proposals have merit . . . and are in keeping with a long history of prudent improvements to the military criminal justice system.

Reform JAG

In addition to those substantive reforms to the current system, Congress should look at a key structural reform to the Judge Advocate General's (JAG) Corps—those military lawyers responsible for prosecuting and defending cases in courts-martial. That long-term structural improvement to the military justice system would preserve the central role of the commander in the military justice process and would create a litigation career track for JAGs in each branch of service.

This will allow those JAGs that choose such a path to fully leverage the ample training they receive. The combined JAG Corps have done an admirable job in providing litigation training, including sexual assault training, to military prosecutors and defense counsel, even when compared to their civilian counterparts. By establishing career tracks for military prosecutors and defense counsel, JAG litigators would be better suited to providing better legal services to victims and defendants alike in the military and align themselves structurally with best practices in the civilian bar.

Arbitrarily taking commanders out of the business of enforcing good order and discipline within their ranks is not the solution to bettering the military's criminal justice system.

A career litigation track will allow victims of sexual assault to work with experienced military prosecutors who have accumulated years of experience, much like their civilian counterparts. Defendants would be represented by learned defense counsel who have handled years of misdemeanor cases, and lower-level felonies, before graduating to sexual assault cases.

The global nature of our armed forces and the complex world in which we live, where law, rules, and regulations govern much of what we do, requires that each service have qualified, fully deployable JAGs. The demand for highly trained uniformed attorneys to defend and prosecute courts-martial is constant. Today's courts-martial, especially felonies, are more complicated to prosecute and defend than in years past.

The military justice system is similar to but distinctly different from its civilian cousin, and it revolves around the concept of enforcing good order and discipline in the armed forces. Arbitrarily taking commanders out of the business of enforcing good order and discipline within their ranks is not the solution to bettering the military's criminal justice system. Rather, the prudent way to improve the military justice system is to build upon the current system, adopt those policies that enhance the delivery of services to victims and defendants alike, and develop career litigation tracks for military prosecutors and defense counsel.

Improvement, Not Radical Change, Is Needed

The Congress of the United States has played a key role in the military justice system. Military justice within our armed forces predates the formation of the country itself. Disciplinary and criminal codes from the armed services were implemented by Presidential Executive Order through the Manual for Courts-Martial (MCM). In the past 50 years, Congress has formalized those rules and procedures through statute in a thoughtful and methodical manner, with a keen appreciation for the fact that the military justice system is uniquely calibrated to support the mission of the military.

For the past few years, Congress has been focused on the issue of sexual assault in the military. In recent months, there have been congressional hearings, legislative proposals, debates, and an ongoing dialogue about how to address this issue. The House has passed key reforms to the existing system in its version of the National Defense Authorization Act (NDAA), and the Senate will take up a variety of reform amendments this fall when it votes on the Senate NDAA. Some of the House and Senate proposals have merit and are in keeping with a long history of prudent improvements to the military criminal justice system.

Senator Kirsten Gillibrand (D-NY), on the other hand, proposes a radical restructuring of the current system by eliminating the power of convening authorities to refer cases to courts-martial. Her proposal is a risky scheme that will ultimately harm victims and undermine justice, good order, and discipline in the armed forces.

The debate over how to address sexual assault in the military has thus far lacked appreciation for the unique historical purposes and features of the military justice system and has failed to include an objective analysis of how this system compares to its civilian counterparts. Upon introducing these considerations, it becomes clear that making prudent improvements to the existing system will better serve all parties concerned, including victims and those accused of sexual assault.

Organizations to Contact

The editors have compiled the following list of organizations concerned with the issues debated in this book. The descriptions are derived from materials provided by the organizations. All have publications or information available for interested readers. The list was compiled on the date of publication of the present volume; names, addresses, phone and fax numbers, and e-mail and Internet addresses may change. Be aware that many organizations take several weeks or longer to respond to inquiries, so allow as much time as possible.

American Civil Liberties Union (ACLU)
125 Broad St., 18th Floor, New York, NY   10004-2400
(212) 549-2500
e-mail: aclu@aclu.org
website: www.aclu.org

The American Civil Liberties Union (ACLU) is a national organization that champions American civil rights. The organization maintains the position that government expediency and national security should not compromise fundamental civil liberties. Its website includes many posts, discussions, and reports on sexual assault in the military.

Center for American Progress (CAP)
1333 H St. NW, 10th Floor, Washington, DC   20005
(202) 682-1611 • fax: (202) 682-1867
e-mail: progress@americanprogress.org
website: www.americanprogress.org

Founded in 2003, the Center for American Progress (CAP) is a progressive think tank that researches, formulates, and advocates for a bold, progressive public policy agenda. The Center's aim is to restore America's global leadership; develop clean, alternative energies that support a sustainable environment; create economic growth and economic opportunities for all

Americans; and advocate for universal health care. CAP scholars provide analyses of significant legal decisions and issues, as well as a wide range of books on legal, political, and public policy issues. The CAP website posts informational videos and video discussions, information on upcoming events, interactive maps and quizzes, commentary on topical issues, and a listing of publications by CAP scholars, as well as a number of articles and blog posts on the issue of sexual assault in the US military.

Family Research Institute (FRI)
PO Box 62640, Colorado Springs, CO 80962-2640
(303) 681-3113
website: www.familyresearchinst.org

The Family Research Institute (FRI), a nonprofit scientific and educational corporation, works to preserve America's historic moral framework and the traditional family. FRI produces scientific data on pressing social issues—especially homosexuality—in an effort to promote traditional policies. The group publishes a monthly newsletter, *Family Research Report*, back issues of which are available online. The website also provides special reports, published articles, and pamphlets on the causes and the effects of homosexuality. The organization has published material arguing that gay service members contribute to the problem of sexual assault in the military.

The Heritage Foundation
214 Massachusetts Ave. NE, Washington, DC 20002-4999
(202) 546-4400 • fax: (202) 546-8328
e-mail: info@heritage.org
website: www.heritage.org

The Heritage Foundation is a research and educational institute that promotes conservative public policies based on the principles of free enterprise, limited government, individual freedom, traditional American values, and a strong national defense. Its website includes policy briefs on US agriculture, the economy, health care, the federal budget and spending, labor, retirement, and social security, as well as international trade policy and economic freedom. It has published a number of posts and reports arguing the sexual assault in the military should be solved through the chain of command rather than civilian courts.

Military Rape Crisis Center (MRCC)

PO Box 45336, Phoenix, AZ 85064
(802) 578-4769
e-mail: Panayiota@stopmilitaryrape.org
website: http://militaryrapecrisiscenter.org

The Military Rape Crisis Center (MRCC) strives to unite agencies engaged in the elimination of sexual violence in the US Armed Forces. MRCC provides case management, victim advocacy, support groups, education, research, and training. It is survivor-run and its services are available to active duty, reserves, National Guard service members, and veterans. Its website includes news reports, information about legislation, and other resources for victims of sexual violence in the military.

Palm Center

University of California, Santa Barbara, CA 93106-9420
(805) 893-5664
website: www.palmcenter.org

The Palm Center, a research initiative of San Francisco State University's Department of Political Science, is committed to sponsoring state-of-the-art scholarship to enhance the quality of public dialogue about critical and controversial issues of the day. For the past decade, the Palm Center's research on sexual minorities in the military has been published in leading social scientific journals. The Palm Center seeks to be a resource for university-affiliated as well as independent scholars, students, journalists, opinion leaders, and members of the public. The Palm Center has published research supporting the inclusion of gays and lesbians in the military, and also researches issues of sexual violence in the military.

Rape, Abuse and Incest National Network (RAINN)

1220 L St. NW, Suite 505, Washington, DC 20005
(202) 544-3556
e-mail: info@rainn.org
website: www.rainn.org

Rape, Abuse and Incest National Network (RAINN) is the nation's largest anti-sexual violence organization and was named one of "America's 100 Best Charities" by *Worth* magazine. RAINN created and operates the National Sexual Assault Hotline in partnership with more than eleven hundred local rape crisis centers across the country and operates the DoD Safe Helpline for the Department of Defense. RAINN also carries out programs to prevent sexual violence, help victims, and ensure that rapists are brought to justice. Its website includes news reports, press releases, and information about sexual violence.

Service Women's Action Network (SWAN)

(646) 569-5200
website: www.servicewomen.org

The mission of the Service Women's Action Network (SWAN) is to transform military culture by securing equal opportunity and freedom to serve without discrimination, harassment, or assault, and to reform veterans' services to ensure high-quality health care and benefits for women veterans and their families. It accomplishes its mission through policy reform, media advocacy, litigation, and community organizing. Its website includes fact sheets, transcripts of testimony, articles, and blogs.

US Department of Defense (DoD)

Office of Public Communication
Assistant Secretary of Defense for Public Affairs
Washington, DC 20310-1400
(703) 428-0711
website: www.defense.gov

The US Department of Defense (DoD) is the agency within the US government charged with providing armed protection for the country as a whole. The department includes all branches of the military and provides a central organizing body for them. DoD's website offers numerous publications and presentations relating to national security and the military, including information related to sexual assault in the military.

US Department of Veterans Affairs (VA)
(202) 461-7600
website: www.va.gov

The US Department of Veterans Affairs (VA) is the agency within the US government that works to serve and honor America's military veterans. It is a military veteran system with cabinet-level status. It supports veterans by providing them with benefits related to such issues as health care and burial. The VA website includes extensive information about the VA's services and veteran affairs. The VA publishes reports, fact sheets, and a magazine, *Vanguard.*

Bibliography

Books

Carolyn B. Allard and Melissa Platt, eds.
Military Sexual Trauma: Current Knowledge and Future Directions. New York: Routledge, 2011.

Helen Benedict
The Lonely Soldier: The Private War of Women Serving in Iraq. Boston: Beacon Press, 2009.

Tanya Biank
Undaunted: The Real Story of America's Servicewomen in Today's Military. New York: Penguin Group, 2013.

Susan Brownmiller
Against Our Will: Men, Women, and Rape. New York: Ballantine Books, 1993.

Helena Carreiras
Gender and the Military: Women in the Armed Forces of Western Democracies. New York: Routledge, 2006.

Jody Clay-Warner and Mary E. Odem, eds.
Confronting Rape and Sexual Assault. Lanham, MD: Rowman & Littlefield, 2013.

Department of Defense, US Military, and Department of Veterans' Affairs
2013 Complete Guide to Military Sexual Assault and Trauma (MST): Senate Hearings, Victim Testimony, Military Justice and Investigations, VA Study Course and Guidelines, Harassment and Rape. US: Progressive Management, 2013.

Mic Hunter
Honor Betrayed: Sexual Abuse in America's Military. Fort Lee, NJ: Barricade Books, 2007.

Cheryl Lawhorne-Scott, Don Philpott, and Jeff Scott
Sexual Assault in the Military: A Guide for Victims and Families. Lanham, MD: Rowman & Littlefield, 2014.

Evelyn Monahan and Rosemary Neidel-Greenlee
A Few Good Women: America's Military Women from World War I to the Wars in Iraq and Afghanistan. New York: Anchor, 2010.

Alexander Nicholson
Fighting to Serve: Behind the Scenes in the War to Repeal "Don't Ask, Don't Tell." Chicago: Chicago Review Press, 2012.

Office of the Inspector General
The Tailhook Report: The Official Inquiry Into the Events of Tailhook '91. New York: St. Martin's Press, 1993.

Rosemarie Skaine
Women in Combat: A Reference Handbook. Santa Barbara, CA: ABC-CLIO, 2011.

Shawn Woodham
Sexual Assault in the Military: Analysis, Response, and Resources. Hauppage, NY: Nova Science, 2013.

Periodicals and Internet Sources

Alan Blinder and Richard A. Oppel, Jr.
"How a Military Sexual Assault Case Foundered," *New York Times*, March 12, 2014.

| Matthew Hay Brown | "Breaking the Silence: Military Sexual Assaults on Males," *Baltimore Sun*, December 14, 2013. |

| James Dao | "In Debate over Military Sexual Assault, Men Are Overlooked Victims," *New York Times*, January 23, 2013. |

| Amy Davidson | "What Gillibrand Got Wrong About Military-Sexual Assault," *New Yorker*, March 7, 2014. |

| Saudi Garcia | "Women in Combat: Military Must Prioritize Sexual Assault Prevention," PolicyMic, March 10, 2013. www.policymic.com. |

| Dahr Jamail | "Military Sexual Abuse 'Staggering,'" Al Jazeera, December 23, 2010. www.aljazeera.com. |

| Kelly Kennedy | "Military Women Say Sexual Assault and Harassment Remain," *USA Today*, July 25, 2013. |

| Karen McVeigh | "Reports of Military Sexual Assault Rise Sharply, Pentagon Figures Show," *Guardian*, November 7, 2013. |

| Patrick J. Murphy | "Why Senator Gillibrand Is Right About Military Sexual Assault," MSNBC, June 17, 2013. www.msnbc.com. |

| Jay Newton-Small | "Senate Passes Bill Tightening Regs on Sexual Assault in the Military," *Time*, March 10, 2014. |

Julia Pollak   "What Politicians Don't Say About
                            the Military's Sexual Assault
                            'Epidemic,'" Breitbart, November 24,
                            2013. www.breitbart.com.

Lindsay Rosenthal   "5 Myths About Military Sexual
and Katie Miller   Assault," Center for American
                            Progress, June 6, 2013. www
                            .americanprogress.org.

Rowan   "False Reports Outpace Sex Assaults
Scarborough   in the Military," *Washington Times*,
                            May 12, 2013.

Sara Sorcher   "How the Military's 'Bro' Culture
                            Turns Women into Targets," *Atlantic*,
                            September 9, 2013.

Mark Thompson   "The Roots of Sexual Abuse in the
                            Military," *Time*, May 17, 2013.

Kayla Williams   "Seven Misconceptions About
                            Military Sexual Assault," Daily Beast,
                            June 4, 2013. www.thdailybeast.com.

Mary Elizabeth   "This Is How You Talk About
Williams   Military Sexual Abuse," *Salon*, June
                            13, 2013. www.salon.com.

Patricia Zengerle   "U.S. Defense Officials Report Slow
                            Progress in Sex Assault Battle,"
                            Reuters, February 26, 2014. www
                            .reuters.com.

Index

WITHDRAWN

CPSIA information can be obtained
at www.ICGtesting.com
Printed in the USA
FFOW05n1301280115

9 780737 771886